Googlies, Nutmegs & Bogeys

Googlies, Nutmegs & Bogeys

The Origins of Peculiar Sporting Lingo

BOB WILSON

ICON BOOKS

Published in the UK in 2006 by
Icon Books Ltd, The Old Dairy,
Brook Road, Thriplow,
Cambridge SG8 7RG
email: info@iconbooks.co.uk
www.iconbooks.co.uk

Sold in the UK, Europe, South Africa and Asia by
Faber & Faber Ltd, 3 Queen Square,
London WC1N 3AU
or their agents

Distributed in the UK, Europe, South Africa and Asia by
TBS Ltd, TBS Distribution Centre, Colchester Road
Frating Green, Colchester CO7 7DW

Published in Australia in 2006 by
Allen & Unwin Pty Ltd,
PO Box 8500, 83 Alexander Street,
Crows Nest, NSW 2065

Distributed in Canada by
Penguin Books Canada,
90 Eglinton Avenue East, Suite 700,
Toronto, Ontario M4P 2YE

ISBN-10: 1-84046-774-6
ISBN-13: 978-1840467-74-1

Typesetting and design by Simmons Pugh

Printed and bound in the UK by
Cromwell Press

About the author

Born in Chesterfield, Bob Wilson found success playing in goal at school and gained England schoolboy honours in 1957. After qualifying as a physical education teacher at Loughborough College, he signed for Arsenal in 1963. He made more than 300 first-team appearances, helping the Gunners win the European Fairs Cup in 1970 and, one year later, the coveted League Championship and FA Cup 'double'. He also became the first English-born player to be capped for Scotland.

In 1974, he embarked on a second career in sports journalism for BBC Television. He presented *Football Focus* for twenty years and was also a regular presenter of *Match of the Day*, *Grandstand*, *Sportsnight* and *Breakfast Sport*. In August 1994, he was lured to the rival channel to be ITV's main football presenter.

An FA Full Badge Coach since 1967, he specialised in the coaching of goalkeepers for 28 years. During that time, the goalkeepers at Arsenal, Queens Park Rangers, Southampton, Tottenham and Luton benefited from his training methods. He ran his own Goalkeeping School for youngsters from 1982 until 1995. He coached the keepers at Arsenal including Pat Jennings and David Seaman.

He has been Chairman of the London Football Coaches Association since 1988. In 1989, he was awarded an honorary degree by Loughborough University for services to football. In 1997 he was appointed to the Board of Governors of the University of Hertfordshire. More recently, he was awarded honorary doctorates by the University of Derby in 2000 and Middlesex University in 2004.

He has written many books on football, mainly involving goalkeeping. These include his history of goalkeeping, *You've Got To Be Crazy* (1989), and his autobiography, *Behind the Network* (2003).

In August 1999, he and his wife Megs launched the Willow Foundation (see page 1), a charity in memory of their daughter Anna who died in December 1998. Bob and Megs have two sons: John, a radio journalist, and Robert, a photographer.

CONTENTS

The Willow Foundation 1

Introduction 2

Addicks 4
albatross 5
All Blacks 6
Amen Corner 8
Annie's room 10
autobus 11
badminton 12
bagel job 13
bails 14
Ball of the Century 15
Barbarians 17
beamer 18
bed and breakfast 19
Bhoys 20
Big Easy 21
birdie 22
Black Cats 23
bodyline 25
bogey 26
bonspiel 27
brassie 28
Brockton Blockbuster 29

broom wagon 31
bumper 32
Bunsen 33
Burlington Bertie 34
Burma Road 35
caddie 36
Calamity Jane 37
Calcutta Cup 38
cap 40
carpet 41
carreau 42
catch a crab 43
chin music 44
Chinaman 45
Claret Jug 46
cocked hat 47
cockpit 48
corridor of uncertainty 49
cow corner 50
coxswain 51
cricket 52
Croke Park 54
croquet 55
Cruyff turn 56
curling 57
Derby 58
deuce 59
devil's number 60
Doctor 61

domestique	62
doosra	63
dormie	64
dot ball	65
duck	66
Duckworth-Lewis method	67
eagle	68
Eau Rouge	69
Eisenhower Tree	70
Eskimo roll	71
flipper	72
fore	73
Fosbury flop	74
furlong	75
Garryowen	76
Gaylord flip	77
Golden Bear	78
golden goal	79
golf	80
googly	82
Greco-Roman	83
Grand Prix	84
Grand Slam	85
Green Jacket	87
gully	88
Gunners	89
haka	91
hand of God	92
hat-trick	94

haymaker 95
Hell Bunker 96
hockey 97
jockey 98
King of the Mountains 99
lanterne rouge 100
lacrosse 101
links 102
Lions 103
Little Master 104
local derby 105
Lord's 107
Louisville Lip 108
love 110
madhouse 111
Madison 112
maiden 113
mankad 114
marathon 116
mashie niblick 117
Masters 118
Michelle 119
Milky Bar Kid 120
mulligan 121
Nelson 123
nightwatchman 124
Nine Dart 126
nineteenth hole 127
nutmeg 128

oche 129

octopush 130

Old Firm 131

on the hoof 132

on the rivet 133

outjump the hill 134

out of the screws 135

Oval 136

pair of spectacles 137

Palooka 138

par 139

Pigeon 140

pits 141

pole position 142

pool 143

popping crease 144

Postage Stamp 145

Pumas 146

pyjama cricket 147

Queensberry Rules 148

rabbit 149

rabbit punch 150

Rae's Creek 151

Rawalpindi Express 152

real tennis 153

red card 154

Red Devils 156

ring 158

Road Hole 159

rope-a-dope 160

scorpion kick 161

show the bowler the maker's name 162

silly point 164

slam-dunk smash 165

sledging 166

snooker 168

soccer 169

southpaw 170

squash 171

Stableford 172

steeplechase 173

sticky dog 174

stumps 175

stymie 176

sweeper 178

sweet science 179

Toffeemen 180

total football 182

Valley of Sin 183

Vardon grip 184

Wallabies 185

Whispering Death 186

yellow jersey 187

yips 188

yorker 189

zooter 190

Index 192

The Willow Foundation

Royalties from the sale of this book will go to the Willow Foundation.

This Foundation is a national charity dedicated to providing quality of life and quality of time for seriously ill young adults (aged 16–40) through the provision of special days. The Foundation defines seriously ill as any condition that is life-threatening. To date, special days have been organised for young adults living with, among other conditions: cancer, motor neurone disease, cystic fibrosis, heart disease, organ failure and muscular dystrophy. The aim of any special day is to offer time out from treatment and allow seriously ill young adults to spend quality time with friends and/or family while pursuing an activity they all enjoy. Each special day is entirely of the applicant's choosing and is organised in meticulous detail. The Foundation funds every aspect of the chosen special day. For some, a special day is their last chance to fulfil a dream. For others, it is the opportunity to return some normality back into their lives. But for all, a special day creates precious memories for the future. Established by former Arsenal and Scotland goalkeeper and TV presenter, Bob Wilson, and his wife Megs, the Willow Foundation is a lasting memorial to their daughter, Anna, who died of cancer aged 31.

To find out more about the charity please go to: www.willowfoundation.org.uk

Introduction

For as long as I can recall, sport has featured in my life, whether simply as a hobby and interest, or as my chosen profession. I come from a sporting family, my Scottish dad being an accomplished cricketer, golfer and footballer, in that order. My four brothers and one sister all found a sport or sports in which they achieved success. Like me they also learned that, as in life, you win, lose or draw along the way, accompanied by huge ups and downs, laughter and tears. I was nicknamed 'Supergame-Rottengame', such were my mood swings following victory and defeat.

Once my dad had, more or less, ordered me to get a 'proper job first' rather than allow me to sign professional forms for Manchester United, I turned to Loughborough College, the leading seat of Sports Education in the country. As soon as I'd qualified as a sports teacher, I rekindled my ambition to play football at the highest level. Arsenal FC became my home and for twelve years as goalkeeper and 28 years as a specialised goalkeeping coach my hunger for success was nourished. After my football-playing career had ended, and alongside my coaching, I was lucky enough to become the first professional sportsman to present all BBC TV's major sports programmes – *Grandstand*, *Sportsnight* and *Match of the Day* – as well as World Cup finals and the Olympic Games.

My fascination with all things sporting has been inherent from day one, and learning the origins and meanings of the terminology attached to particular sports has been a pleasurable journey. *Googlies, Nutmegs and Bogeys* covers the funny, the obscure and the downright bizarre terms associated with the sporting world. Many of the words you'll be familiar with, some you may never have heard before ... in either case, these definitions are sure to provide some surprises and raise a few smiles along the way. The wealth of sporting terms from across the world made selecting them extremely difficult – hopefully some of those that had to be left out this time around might make it into a second volume.

Addicks

[football] – *a nickname for Charlton Athletic FC*

Some believe that this name is simply a corruption of *Athletic*, although the more popular and likely theory is that it derives from the word *haddock*; the club was formed by a group of teenagers in 1905 and sponsored in its early years by a local fish-monger named Arthur Bryan, while they settled at their ground, the Valley. After matches, he would give both the home and away teams a fish supper. The story goes that if Charlton lost, they would have cod, but if they won, they would dine on the more expensive *'addock*, which then produced the nickname *Addicks*.

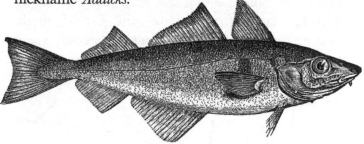

albatross

[golf] – *a score of three under par on a hole*

The term *albatross* came into use by golfers in the late 1930s in the UK and later across Europe, developing from the established **birdie** and **eagle**, which had been in use since earlier in the century. Most golfers never achieve an albatross in their entire career, as indicated by the rarity of bird chosen to represent this feat. Ab Smith, American co-creator of the term 'birdie' in 1899, referred to it as a *double eagle*, the name which most American golfers still use today.

All Blacks

[rugby union] – *the nickname for the New Zealand national team*

In 1905, the New Zealand rugby team made their first tour of Britain. They embarked on the tour as *The Originals* but returned as the *All Blacks*. There are two theories for this.

After one match in which they beat Hartlepool 63-0, J.A. Buttery of the *Daily Mail* referred to them as the *All Backs*, based on the ability of their forwards to play with the speed and precision of any of the backs. When they went on to their next tour match in Taunton to play Somerset County, the whole town was covered with posters welcoming the 'All Blacks', with an extra 'l' in it due to a printer's error. The *Daily Mail* picked up the incorrect name, using it again in an article announcing the team's tour schedule through

Ireland. Billy Wallace, a player on the tour, recounts that due to the article, many people turned out to catch a glimpse of the team, 'and when they saw us go past said: "Bejasus, they are as white as ourselves, as white as ourselves."'

However, the more likely and commonly held view is that the name originated from another article by Buttery, in which he referred to 'the visit of the All Blacks, so dubbed because of their sombre football garb. The only colour not black was the silver fern on the left breast and the white of their bootlaces.'

Amen Corner

[golf] – *holes 11, 12 and 13 at the Augusta National Golf Club, Georgia*

A term coined in a *Sports Illustrated* article in 1958 by journalist Herbert Warren Wind. He used it for the second half of hole 11, all of hole 12 and the first half of hole 13, and the term was his way of summing up where all the critical action had taken place in the *Masters* that year.

It was the year of the Masters that saw Arnold Palmer win his first Major, with the help of a ruling in the final round that incensed runner-up Ken Venturi – to such an extent that he still challenges it to this day. The tournament's official description of the events is as follows:

Saturday evening in 1958, heavy rains soaked the course. For Sunday's round, a local rule was adopted allowing a player whose ball was embedded to lift and drop it without penalty. Sunday on No. 12, Arnold Palmer hit his ball over the green and the ball embedded in the steep bank behind it. Being uncertain about the applicability of the local rule, the official on the hole and Palmer agreed that the ball should be played as it lay and that Palmer could play a second ball which he dropped. Palmer holed out for a 5 with the original ball and a 3 with the second ball. The committee was asked to decide if the local rule was applicable and if so, which score should count.

*At No. 13, still unsure of what his score was at 12, Palmer sank an 18-foot putt for **eagle** 3. When he was playing No. 15, Palmer was told his drop at 12 was proper and that his score on the hole was 3, leading to his first major victory.*

So *Amen* conveys how that *corner* of the course helped to determine the result, effectively concluding the tournament, as it does a prayer. But it's thought that Wind also chose it to suggest the seemingly miraculous way in which Palmer played those holes that day. Reputedly he took the name from an old jazz song, 'Shouting at Amen Corner'.

Annie's room

[darts] – *a score of double one*

The phrase 'he's up in Annie's room' gained common usage during the First World War, as a dismissive answer to a question about the whereabouts of a particular soldier. It suggested the missing soldier was where he shouldn't have been – up to no good with Annie upstairs. Over time, *Annie's room* found its way into the phraseology of darts, and was applied in the same way: double one is not where a player should be. It usually means he's had plenty of throws at higher doubles before following the inevitable path to double one, and therefore should have finished the game long before ending up on the most difficult double.

autobus

[cycling] – *a group of riders who fall behind, but stick together to help each other finish inside the time limit for that stage*

Typically, an *autobus* – so called because of the group's slow pace and the number of people in it – will form on a mountain stage of a race. The group is composed of sprinters and flat-specialists but, most importantly, includes a *bus driver* – a cyclist with the ability to determine a pace that minimises the energy the group has to expend, but quick enough to get the autobus home within the cut-off time. If they fail to do this, they hope that by remaining in a big enough group, the officials will have to let them continue in the race – otherwise too many riders would be eliminated. This doesn't always work, however.

Otherwise known as the *gruppetto*, Italian for *little group* or *laughing group*.

badminton

[badminton] – *a racquet sport*

The sport's beginnings date back over 2,000 years: it was played, in its original form, in ancient Greece, China, Egypt and India. Throughout the Middle Ages, it came to be known as *battledore and shuttlecock*, in which children would hit a small feathered cork back and forth with paddles covered in taut leather. The modern game was introduced to England in the 19th century by returning British army officers who developed the game while serving in India. Soon after, the sport took its name from the Duke of Beaufort's country house in South Gloucestershire, *Badminton* House, where many games were played during the 1870s. The first official rules were drawn up in 1873.

bagel job

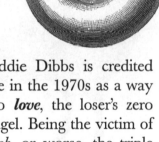

[tennis] – *a set won 6-0*

American tennis player Eddie Dibbs is credited with introducing this phrase in the 1970s as a way of describing a set won to **love**, the loser's zero supposedly resembling a bagel. Being the victim of the dreaded double *bagel job*, or worse, the triple bagel job, is every player's nightmare.

bails

[cricket] – *the crosspieces bridging the stumps*

The English adopted the word *bail* from the French in the 16th century to describe the movable horizontal part of the small *wicket* (gate) used as an entrance to a sheepfold. In early versions of cricket, this gate was often used as a target for the bowler – the equivalent of today's **stumps**, which as we know, also hold up the *bails* – the two small pieces of wood which were officially introduced to the game in 1817.

Ball of the Century

[cricket] – *the name given to Shane Warne's first-ever Ashes delivery*

In 1993, a young and unknown leg-spinner named Shane Warne made his Ashes debut at Old Trafford. In the tour matches leading up to the first Test, Australian captain Allan Border had opted to keep Warne's talents under wraps, encouraging him to bowl deliberately innocuously and allow the opposition to treat his bowling with the appropriate contempt for a newcomer.

That all changed with his first-ever ball in Ashes cricket. After a slow and short run-up, he released what appeared to be a standard leg-break to the facing right-handed Mike Gatting. Initially, it travelled straight through the air, but gradually the prodigious spin on the ball made it drift to the right, dip suddenly, and finally pitch well outside the leg stump.

Gatting had thrust his bat and pad forward and down the leg side in the normal manner adopted to defend a leg-break of this kind. As the ball had pitched outside the leg stump there was no danger of him being out lbw – and if the ball moved more off the pitch than expected, then the bat would be in place as defence. Needless to say, this was no normal delivery. Having drifted down the leg side, the ball bit off the pitch and moved immeasurably the other way. The deviation of the ball was far greater than normally seen on a Test pitch, especially in England, and it sailed past Gatting's pad and bat to hit his off stump. Memorably, Gatting stood and stared for several seconds in utter disbelief at the impossibility of it all before he finally accepted his fate and headed for the pavilion.

It was so utterly brilliant that the *Gatting Ball*, as it is otherwise known, was immediately labelled by the media as the *Ball of the Century* – an accolade very few have seen fit to contest.

Barbarians

[rugby union] – *an international invitational rugby club but with no ground or clubhouse*

The *Barbarian Football Club* was the brainchild of William Percy Carpmael from Blackheath, London. Its intended purpose was to bring together players from across the world to spread good fellowship throughout the game, and the team continues to this day. Carpmael formed the idea for the club while on tour to the north of England in 1890, late one evening over an oyster supper in Leuchters restaurant, at the Alexandra Hotel in Bradford – but the later choice of name remains a mystery. Some believe that it was named by a classics scholar who thought it 'dignified by the famous victory of Arminius over Varius and his legions in Germany some two thousand years ago', but past president of the club, Emile de Lissa, thought *Barbarian* was more likely chosen 'in defiance of those who would style all rugby players as just that'.

beamer

[cricket] – *a fast and dangerous full-toss delivery that reaches the batsman at head height*

Reputedly this delivery, when bowled deliberately, was invented by a fast bowler at Cambridge University because of his frustration at the slow and innocuous pitch at Fenners, the team's home ground. Achieving little success, he decided to upset the batsmen by bowling at their heads. Long before sightscreens were introduced, Fenners was notorious for the difficulty batsmen faced in detecting the flight of the ball due to the dark background of trees.

The obvious suggestion for this delivery's name is as a derivation of *beam*, meaning something straight and direct. However, it might possibly have been borrowed from the biblical phrase *a beam in one's eye*, which indicates that you are more at fault than those with only a splinter in theirs.

bed & breakfast

[darts] – *a score of 26*

A relatively common total from three darts as a result of hitting 20, 5 and 1 when aiming for treble 20. It's also known as the *two and six*, from which it derives its name: two shillings and sixpence was the traditional cost of a night's lodging early in the 20th century.

The term is often abbreviated to simply *breakfast*. If you get a treble 20, treble 5 and treble 1 in the same throw, then you've got yourself a *champagne breakfast*.

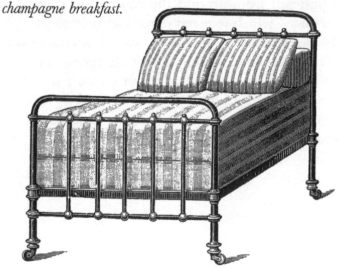

Bhoys

[football] – *a nickname for Celtic FC*

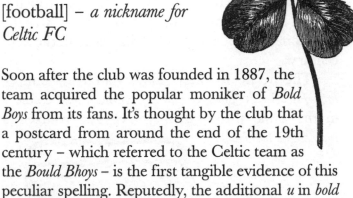

Soon after the club was founded in 1887, the team acquired the popular moniker of *Bold Boys* from its fans. It's thought by the club that a postcard from around the end of the 19th century – which referred to the Celtic team as the *Bould Bhoys* – is the first tangible evidence of this peculiar spelling. Reputedly, the additional *u* in *bold* and *h* in *boys* was an attempt to indicate the Irish pronunciation of the phrase. The new spelling stuck, but over time it became abbreviated to simply the *Bhoys*, and the name stands to this day.

Big Easy

[golf] – *a popular nickname for professional golfer Ernie Els*

'Perhaps the epitome of the slow-motion swing is the *Big Easy*, Ernie Els. What a marvel is the power that's produced by that big, slow-motion arc', wrote Dr Tom Dorsel in a *Golf Illustrated* article in February 2001. This is not the first use of the nickname by any means, but it does help to illustrate how, along with his easygoing demeanour, the 6′3″ South African gained it.

Recently the golf world has seen the emergence of young female phenomenon Michelle Wie. Comparisons have been made between the styles of Els and Wie due to her 6′0″ stature and her elegant and relaxed swing. This led Tom Lehman to give her the nickname, the *Big Wiesy*.

birdie

[golf] – *a score of one under par on a hole*

In 19th-century American slang, the term 'bird' was used to describe anything good. Reputedly, *birdie* originated in golf in 1899, during a game between Ab Smith, his brother William Smith and George Crump at the Country Club in Atlantic City. On the *par*-4 second hole, Ab Smith hit his second shot to within inches of the hole and exclaimed he had hit 'a bird of a shot'. He suggested that if one of them played a hole in one under par, then that person should receive double the money from the others, and all agreed. He duly holed his putt to win with what they called, from that point on, a birdie.

Black Cats

[football] – *a nickname for Sunderland AFC*

There are various links between the club and the *black cat* stretching back over the last 200 years. In 1805, a nearby gun battery on the River Wear was renamed the Black Cat battery after a number of workers heard a mysterious wailing that turned out to be a black cat trapped inside the factory. Then there's a photograph from 1905, a hundred years later, of F.W. Taylor, the club chairman, with a black cat sitting on a football next to him – and three years later, in 1908, the black cat crept into a full team photograph.

Before long, black cats were featuring in the match day programme and in club-related cartoons in the local paper. For the FA Cup Final in 1937, many fans wore a specially made black-cat tie-pin to hold their red-and-white buttonhole in place. After the same final, the press made much of twelve-year-old Billy Morris and his black kitten, which sat in his pocket at Wembley throughout that game – supposedly bringing the team sufficient luck to come from behind and beat Preston 3-1. For years, a black cat also lived at Roker Park, where it

was looked after by the club, and its
arrival sparked a long winning streak.

Despite all this, it's only recently that the
name was properly adopted by the club. It
has had a number of nicknames in its
history, including the *Roker Men* and the
Rokerites, but the move from Roker Park in
1997 left these redundant. It's only now, fully
ensconced at the Stadium of Light – with
their match-day mascots Samson and
Delilah – that Sunderland have truly become
known as the *Black Cats*.

bodyline

[cricket] – *fast bowling aimed at the batsman's body*

Also known as *fast leg theory*, this tactic was in use for some time before England's tour of 1932–33 when it was most infamously used, and named *bodyline* by the press. Douglas Jardine, the English captain on the tour, instructed his fast bowlers to bowl directly at the bodies of Australian batsmen in the hope of them directing easy catches to a stacked and close leg-side field. Although this tactic managed to keep the brilliant Don Bradman in check and consequently won England the Ashes, it caused several injuries to the Australian batsmen and became a full-blown political furore. 'I've not travelled 6,000 miles to make friends. I'm here to win the Ashes', was Jardine's response.

The laws of cricket came under scrutiny and saw several changes over the following decade to prevent another *Bodyline Series*, as it came to be known.

bogey

[golf] – *a score of one more than par on a hole*

I always have plenty of *bogeys* on my card. The name for these little blighters originated with the character called the *Bogey Man* in a popular British song from the 1890s. Later he became known as *Colonel Bogey*, and with this the song became 'The Colonel Bogey March'. Colonel Bogey was an elusive figure that hid himself wherever and whenever he could: 'I'm the Bogey Man, catch me if you can' he teased. Initially, bogey meant the same as *par*, i.e. the ideal score for the hole. As a result, and as suggested by the lyric 'catch me if you can', golfers chased the Bogey Man on the course in search of the perfect score.

In the early part of the 20th century, however, the meaning of the term changed. According to other lyrics in the song, the Bogey Man was very much someone to fear, so bogey became one over par, i.e. a score to be avoided.

bonspiel

[curling] – *a tournament*

Bonspiels are **curling** tournaments that originated in Scotland on frozen freshwater lochs. Outdoor bonspiels are now a very rare sight in the country as a result of global warming. The word is an amalgamation of the French *bon*, meaning *good*, and German *spiel*, meaning *game*, and is thought to have been inherited by the Scots from the invading Vikings, who invented their own language as they rampaged across Europe.

brassie

[golf] – *an old equivalent to a 2-wood*

This was a wooden club with more loft than a driver but less than the *spoon* (the equivalent of the 3-wood, so called because of its slightly hollowed face). The *brassie* takes its name from its fitted brass sole plate.

Brockton Blockbuster

[boxing] – *a nickname for Rocky Marciano*

The first boxer I remember admiring as a young boy was Rocky Marciano. Weighing-in at a sizeable twelve pounds at his birth on 1 September 1923, Rocky was born and raised in Brockton, Massachusetts. He contracted a virulent strain of pneumonia at 18 months of age, and his doctor claimed it was only his particularly strong constitution that kept him alive. At fifteen, playing baseball for his local team, he hit a home run out of Brockton's James Edgar Playground – which reputedly landed on the front porch of a house 330 feet away. At 24, he embarked on a career as a professional boxer. After winning 37 fights by knockout, he fought Jersey Joe Walcott for the Heavyweight Championship of the World on 23 September 1953. Despite being knocked down in the first round and being behind on points for the first seven, Rocky knocked out Walcott with what's regarded as one of the most devastating punches in boxing history – a punch he thereafter referred to as his *Susie Q.*

The *Brockton Blockbuster* defended his title six times, the only world heavyweight champion to retire with a perfect record. His entire professional record of 49 fights, 49 wins and 43 knockouts may never be matched. It's not difficult to see how he acquired the name.

broom wagon

[cycling] – *a support vehicle that follows and picks up riders that retire in a stage race*

Introduced at the Tour de France after mountain stages were added in 1910, the vehicle acquired the name based on its task of 'sweeping-up' exhausted riders who fall too far behind in the race. It sometimes has broom bristles attached to the front bumper or a whole broom bolted to the car in a wonderful bit of symbolism that's sadly seen less and less in the modern era. Before entering the broom wagon, the rider must suffer a further humiliation as they have their dossard or back number removed from their jersey by an official. Also known as a sag wagon.

bumper

[cricket] – *a fast and short-pitched
delivery intended to reach the batsman
at chest or head height*

Because of potential danger to batsmen
from this hostile delivery, the laws of
cricket stipulate how frequently it may be
bowled, taking into account the relative
skill of the batsman. *Bumper*, based on the
frequency with which the ball would *bump*
into the batsman, is really a term from the
past – the delivery has acquired the more
self-explanatory name of *bouncer* in recent
times.

Bunsen

[cricket] – *a pitch favourable to spin bowlers*

From the cockney rhyming slang *Bunsen burner*, meaning a *turner*.

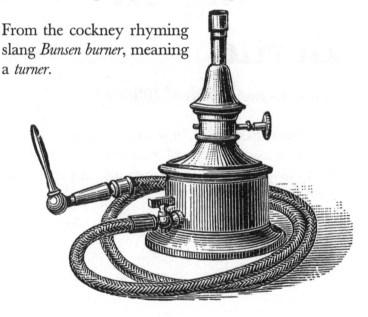

Burlington Bertie

[horse racing] – *odds of 100/30*

The term *Burlington Bertie* comes from the old popular music hall song of the same name. Chosen as rhyming slang, it's sometimes also referred to as *scruffy and dirty*.

Burma Road

[golf] – the famous West Course at Wentworth Golf Club

I love playing this golf course, which has just had a makeover under the guidance of the **Big Easy**. Originally designed by Harry Colt and opened in 1926, *Burma Road* is the most televised course in Britain, playing host to both the World Match Play and the PGA Championship every year. The Ryder Cup was also held there in 1953.

Upon the outbreak of the Second World War, the British army commandeered the club and built an elaborate network of underground bunkers, including a secret headquarters that still lies deep beneath the clubhouse. To prevent enemy aircraft landing on the fairways, the course was allowed to grow wild, but towards the end of the war this was no longer a concern. German POWs from an internment camp in nearby Egham were brought in to clear the vegetation. 'Let this be their Burma Road', one of the British officers reputedly said.

caddie

[golf] – *the person who carries a golfer's clubs and assists with choice of club, reading of greens, etc.*

Caddie comes from the French *cadet* meaning *boy* or *youngest*. Traditionally in France, the youngest sons of aristocratic families would join the army, and it's thought that these military cadets, as they came to be known, would sometimes be used to carry the clubs of Royal golfers; a practice also applied in Scotland upon the return of Queen Mary Stuart in 1561. The word 'cadet' appears in English for the first time in 1610.

In Scottish towns in the 18th century, particularly in and around Edinburgh, there were a large number of men trying to make a living as a porter or messenger, especially by delivering water. As many of these men were ex-army, they came to be known as caddies. There are many references to the carrying of golf clubs by these odd-job men of the time, but it wasn't until the following century that 'caddie' was used almost exclusively for those employed for this task.

Calamity Jane

[golf] – *Bobby Jones's famous putter*

One of the greatest golfers of the early 20th century, and indeed of all time, was Bobby Jones. His putter, with a simple offset blade, was made in 1900 – and was already twenty years old and nicknamed *Calamity Jane* when it was given to Jones in 1920. Jones replaced it in 1926 with a putter made by Spalding, which he called *Calamity Jane II.* He won ten more major championships and retired in 1930 – winning the **Grand Slam** (all four majors in one year, though these are not the same four majors as today's Grand Slam). Jones became a consultant to Spalding, which made many Calamity Jane models between 1932 and 1973. Jones gave Calamity Jane II to the USGA Museum, while the original is held by Augusta National Golf Club.

Calcutta Cup

[rugby union] – *a trophy for which England and Scotland have competed since 1879*

In Calcutta on Christmas Day 1872, two teams of twenty men each, one representing England and the other Scotland, Ireland and Wales, played the first game of rugby football India had ever seen. It was a resounding success and they repeated the fixture the following week. Despite the unsuitable Indian climate, a group of them wanted to establish the game in the country and so, in 1873, formed the Calcutta Rugby Club. It thrived in its first year but gradually members turned to polo and tennis due to, among other things, their greater suitability to the local climate. A number of members also left when they stopped the free bar at the club!

In time, the remaining members decided to disband, but were determined to keep the club alive in some form or other. They withdrew the club's remaining funds from the bank and had them melted down and made into a trophy which they

presented to the Rugby Football Union (RFU) in 1878, on the condition that it be competed for annually. The RFU obliged, deciding it should be contested for by England and Scotland. The first *Calcutta Cup* match, played on 10 March 1879 at Raeburn Place in Edinburgh, ended in a draw. England became the first winners of the trophy when they played on 28 February the following year.

The trophy is still contested to this day, now as part of the Six Nations Championship. In 2004, the governing bodies of rugby in both England and Scotland considered adding an additional Calcutta Cup fixture to the calendar, outside of the Six Nations. They proposed that one nation would have to win both matches to take the trophy from its current holder, but the idea was met with a largely unfavourable reaction and so was dropped.

cap

[football] – *an appearance for a national team*

This term can be used for any sport but, because of its origin, is most closely linked to football. On 10 May 1886, a new concept was approved in the United Kingdom whereby each and every player representing their country would receive a commemorative piece of headgear for an international match. The practice came about as a result of the proposal by the Old Corinthian player N.L. Jackson: 'That all players taking part for England in future international matches be presented with a white silk *cap* with a red rose on the front, these to be termed "International Caps".'

Uniquely, I have England caps (England Schoolboys 1957) and Scottish caps (Full Scottish International 1971–2), and these are among my most prized sporting possessions.

carpet

[horse racing] – *odds of 3/1*

This term derives from criminal slang for a three-month stretch in prison. 33/1 is known as a double carpet.

carreau

[boules] – *throwing and landing your ball directly on top of the winning ball of the opposition, not only knocking theirs away, but also leaving yours in the exact position vacated by the other ball*

This is the most difficult shot in boules – but should you master it, you have a chance in any match. Many players are good at this at home, but the precision required is such that, due to unfamiliar surroundings and additional pressure, it's a much rarer sight in competition. Its name is thought to derive from the fighting term *rester carreau* meaning *to remain on the spot* or *to be laid out cold*.

catch a crab

[rowing] – *to sink the oar too deeply into the water, causing the boat to jolt violently*

This unpleasant moment for a rower is called to *catch a crab* as it feels like a crab has grabbed the blade of the oar under the water. In the worst cases, rowers are thrown from the boat or the boat is even flipped. The first use of the term is unknown.

chin music

[cricket] – *continued fast and short-pitched bowling*

Originally a euphemism for punching someone in the jaw dating back to 19th-century America, it was adopted by the cricketing world in the 1980s to describe the attack of the fast West Indian bowlers of the time. With the likes of Joel Garner and Malcolm Marshall bowling continuously short on the lively Caribbean pitches, the ball flying at 95 mph past the trembling chins of English batsmen was a common sight.

Chinaman

[cricket] – *a ball from an orthodox left-arm wrist-spinner, which turns the opposite way to the normal delivery from this type of bowler (i.e. left to right instead of the usual right to left)*

This term is thought to come from the series between England and the West Indies in 1933. At the Old Trafford Test, Ellis Achong, the West Indian left-arm spinner of Chinese descent, had English batsman Walter Robins stumped by several yards. Reputedly, on returning to the pavilion, Robins exclaimed to the umpire, Joe Hardstaff Snr., 'Fancy being done by a bloody *Chinaman!*', and that's where it started.

Claret Jug

[golf] – *a popular name for the trophy contested annually at the Open Championship*

This is one of the most prized and stylish trophies in sport. Despite its official name of the *Golf Champion Trophy*, the prize acquired the more widely used *Claret Jug*, as that's exactly what it is. Created in 1873 by Mackay Cunningham & Co. of Edinburgh, thanks to a contribution of £10 each from Prestwick, the Royal and Ancient Golf Club of St Andrews, and the Honourable Company of Edinburgh Golfers, it was commissioned and made in the style of elaborate silver jugs used at the time to serve red wine from the famous region of Bordeaux.

cocked hat

[snooker] – *a shot in which the ball hit by the white rebounds off three different cushions towards a middle pocket*

This shot acquired its name based on the trajectory of the shot that, seen from above, resembles an old-fashioned, three-cornered *cocked hat* – a piece of formal headgear worn by particular military, naval and civilian officials from the mid-19th century until the beginning of the Second World War.

cockpit

[motor racing] – *the confined space in which the driver sits to control the car*

The first reference to this term dates back to 1587, when it was used to describe the pit dug to house cockfights. Over the following century, the term was applied to unpleasant places of combat on a more general level. Simultaneously – helped on its way by William Shakespeare, who in *Henry V* used the term to refer to the area around the stage with the lowest level of seating – it began to be used as a general term for sunken or confined spaces. For example, on British Naval vessels in the 17th and 18th centuries, the small, cramped area below deck – used as quarters for junior officers and for treating the wounded during battle – acquired the name, as did the area towards the stern of boats that houses the rudder controls. In this way, the meaning of *cockpit* developed to include any confined space used for control purposes. The term was taken up by pilots during the First World War, before finally being adopted by motor racing in the mid-1930s.

corridor of uncertainty

[cricket] – *a line of delivery just outside off-stump that leaves the batsman uncertain which shot to play*

Former Yorkshire and England batsman Geoffrey Boycott invented this term while commentating on the England tour of the Caribbean in 1990. 'It was a phrase I came up with on the spot', he said, and it's since been adopted by football commentators for the area between the defenders and the goal-keeper when a cross is delivered into the penalty box. In this instance, the *uncertainty* refers to the potential confusion between the players as to who will go for the ball. I hated having to try to deal with a ball delivered in this way. Fumbles by the keeper or own goals by defenders are common when the ball is delivered into the *corridor of uncertainty*.

cow corner

[cricket] – *an area of the field near the boundary between deep midwicket and long-on*

There are several theories for the birth of this cricketing term – and all somewhat unsurprisingly involve cows.

Cow corner is an unconventional fielding position and players are rarely dispatched there, leaving an area safe for cows to graze while matches are being played.

If a fielder is placed there, it's usually specifically in hopes of a catch from a high ball right on the boundary. In the early days of cricket, when pitches were in fields shared with livestock, it's thought that fielders were often too concerned with what they might be treading in to devote their attention to the ball and take the catch.

However, the most likely source of this term is the First XI pitch at Dulwich College where, in the past, there was a corner of a field containing cattle that met that part of the boundary. Captains would dispatch their fielders to what became cow corner.

coxswain

[rowing] – *the only person in the boat who doesn't actually row but is in charge of steering and giving instructions to the rest of the crew instead*

Originally a *coxswain* or *cockswain* was the boy servant or swain in charge of the small *cockleboat* or *cock* that was kept aboard the main ship and used to ferry the captain to and from the shore. The first reference to this dates back to 1463. Over the centuries, it became used for the helmsman of any boat, whatever the size, until it was adopted by the sport of rowing. The abbreviation of *cox* – as is more commonly used today – reputedly came about in the 19th century.

cricket

[cricket] – *a sport played with a ball, bats and wickets by two teams of eleven players*

The sport is perhaps recorded as early as the end of the 12th century, when Joseph of Exeter wrote of a game he called *cricks* being played by both men and women – although there's nothing to prove this was a form of *cricket*. Later, in the household accounts of Edward I for the year 1299, Master John de Leek, chaplain to Edward's son, was paid 100 shillings for organising the 'prince's playing at *creag* and other sports' at Newenden in Kent. Although we can't be certain that this was a type of cricket either, it does seem likely, given that this was in the heartland of cricket's history. This creag and *handyn and handoute* (another early form of cricket) gained popularity through the next few centuries, until the latter was banned by Edward IV in 1477 as he considered it a distraction from the compulsory archery practice that he imposed in order to keep his population ready for any further conflict with France.

There are no other references to the sport until 1597, when in a court proceeding over some disputed land at a school in Guildford, John

Derrick, a 59-year-old coroner, testified that 'hee and several of his fellowes did runne and play there at *creckett* ... for the space of fyfty years and more'. Soon after, the name acquired the spelling that we know today. In 1611, two men from Sussex were prosecuted for playing 'cricket' instead of going to church, and in 1617, when Oliver Cromwell went to London at the age of eighteen, he was said to have 'gained himself the name of Royster' by playing 'football, cricket, cudgelling and wrestling'.

A number of words are considered to be possible sources for the name cricket. From old French there is *criquet* – meaning a type of club – that probably gave its name to the game of **croquet**, and some historians believe that the two sports have a common origin. Another theory is that the name was adopted from the Flemish *krickstoel* – meaning a long, low stool upon which one kneels in church – as a result of its profile being similar to the long, low wickets of two tree stumps and crosspiece used in early cricket. But probably the most likely suggestion is the Old English *cricc* or *cryce* – meaning a staff or shepherd's crook similar to the long, curved bats that were used in early forms of cricket.

Croke Park

[miscellaneous] – *the largest stadium in Ireland*

Home to the Gaelic Athletic Association, *Croke Park* in Dublin is used for Gaelic football, hurling and camogie, has a capacity of 82,300, and is the fourth largest stadium in Europe. It was named in 1913, in honour of Archbishop Thomas Croke, one of the GAA's first patrons. At that stage, it comprised a couple of stands and some grass banks. In 1917, the rubble left from the Easter Rising – a rebellion staged against British rule on Easter Monday 1916 – was used to build the famous *Hill 16* at the railway end of the pitch. Later, on 20 November 1920, as retaliation for the murder of twelve British intelligence officers earlier that day, British police auxiliaries burst into Croke Park during a Dublin–Tipperary football match, firing indiscriminately into the crowd. They killed thirteen spectators and the Tipperary captain, Michael Hogan, who has since had a stand named after him. The day became known as Bloody Sunday.

croquet

[croquet] – *an outdoor game played with a mallet and balls by two to four players*

This game is widely reckoned to have developed from a French pastime popular in the 12th century, called *jeu de mail*. By the 14th century, this had become *paille-maille* in which crude mallets were used to knock balls through hoops made of bent willow branches. By the 17th century an anglicised *pall mall* – with a curved club, a wooden ball, and two hoops – was being popularised in England by the court of Charles II. They played it in St James's Park, and the game gave its name to the nearby street that remains today.

The game lost favour during the 18th century, until it resurfaced as *crooky* in Ireland in the 1830s. Although uncertain, it's thought that the game reached Ireland via French refugees or visiting French nuns. This would corroborate the theory that the term 'croquet' is a derivation of the old French word *croche*, meaning *shepherd's crook*.

Cruyff turn

[football] – *an effective move intended to lose a tracking opponent, whereby the player pretends to pass the ball but drags it back instead, turns the body and accelerates the other way*

This move takes its name from the brilliant three-time European Footballer of the Year, Dutchman Johann Cruyff. He first used it against a bemused Swedish defender during the 1974 World Cup. This was one of the nine World Cup tournaments I worked on during my TV career. I knew Johann and had played against him several times for club and country. I still rank him alongside Pele, Maradona and George Best as the best footballers ever. When he produced this moment of magic, he took our breath away and instantly inspired a new generation of players to replicate it and add to their own skills repertoire.

curling

[curling] – *a sport played on ice with granite stones*

It's a common misconception that the name of this sport comes from the slight and deliberate spin placed on the stone as it's released, causing it to deviate (or curl) from its original straight-line trajectory. In the sport's early years, stones were simply taken from a nearby river, and their natural shape was such that the player had little or no control over them. The word *curling* first appeared in print in a poem by Henry Adamson in Perth, Scotland, in 1620. It derives from the Old English verb *to curr* which means *to growl* – a reference to the noise made by the stones as they slide across the ice. Consequently, the sport was referred to as the *roaring game* – and in Scotland, some still use this name.

Derby

[horse racing] – *a one-mile, four-furlong and ten-yard flat race held annually on the first Saturday in June at Epsom Downs racetrack in Surrey, England*

One day in the late 1770s, while staying in a house opposite Epsom Downs, Sir Charles Bunbury and Edward Smith-Stanley (the twelfth Earl of *Derby*) decided that the unusual contours and beauty of the landscape would make a perfect location to race their three-year-old fillies. So, in 1779, they organised the inaugural race of this category, calling it the *Oaks* after the Earl's nearby Epsom estate.

The following year they introduced another race in which both three-year-old fillies and colts were allowed to race; the idea being that by maintaining the age limit but having horses of both sexes enter, they would be able to establish the best horse of each generation. They flipped a coin to see whom the race would be named after. Needless to say, the Earl won, and so the most prestigious flat race for thoroughbred horses in the world today became the Derby.

deuce

[tennis] – *the score of 40-40*

This comes from the French *à deux de jeu,* indicating that there are two points to play before the game can be won by either player. Initially, the English used the old French spelling and abbreviated it to *à deus,* before modifying it to one syllable: the more easily said *deuce.*

devil's number

[cricket] – *the score of 87, considered unlucky by Australian cricketers*

The Australian equivalent of England's *Nelson*, the *devil's number* is believed to be bad luck as it's 13 runs short of a century. Also, up until 2005, Australia had not lost the Ashes since 1987, so some think that this date played a part. The origin of the superstition is unknown.

Doctor

[cricket] – *the nickname for the cricketing legend W.G. Grace*

Although he made considerably more money from cricket than all his fellow professional players, William Gilbert Grace was officially an amateur player. He was a medical man by profession – on one occasion having to ply his trade on an unfortunate fielder who impaled himself on Old Trafford's boundary fence – hence his nickname the *Doctor*.

Due to the inordinate time he devoted to cricket, however, it was perhaps one of the longest medical trainings in history. Beginning his study as a 19-year-old bachelor, he passed his finals as a father of three in his thirties. He came from a predominantly medical family, who similarly put cricket first – on one occasion his coroner brother put a corpse on ice just so he could attend to it at the close of play.

domestique

[cycling] – *a member of a professional cycling team, whose job is to ride solely for the benefit of the team and team leader, instead of their own glory*

These are used predominantly to dictate the pace of the *peloton* (the main group of riders) during a race, but are called upon in all eventualities. For example, should their team leader suffer a puncture, the *domestique* will wait with them until it's fixed, then cycle to the front in order to create a slipstream and allow the team leader to recover their position. In more extreme circumstances, they may be asked to sacrifice their bicycle should their leader's suffer irreparable damage. Although they do not share the fame of their team colleagues, a good domestique is highly respected within his sport. Sometimes they can achieve fame of their own, however, as Lucien Aimar proved when he supported the illustrious Jacques Anquetil on the 1966 Tour de France, but ended up winning it instead.

Despite *domestique* being the French word for *servant*, the French refer to this member of the team as *porteur d'eau* or *water carrier*.

doosra

[cricket] – *a ball that is the off-spinner's equivalent of a leg-spinner's googly, whereby the top-spinning delivery from the back of the bowler's hand turns away from a right-handed batsman*

This is a Hindi and Urdu word meaning the *second* or *other one*. It's a relatively new development in the game, with Pakistan's Saqlain Mushtaq its first successful practitioner in the mid-to-late 1990s. However, the legality of the *doosra* within the game has been called into question on a number of occasions since its inception, as many believe it's impossible to produce while retaining a legitimate bowling action.

dormie

[golf] – *the situation in matchplay when a player has a lead which equals the number of holes left*

Dormie derives from the French verb *dormir* meaning *to sleep*. The term was adopted based on the thought that a player can relax or even go to sleep without fear of losing the match. Although this is true, a halved match can sometimes feel more like a loss, as Mark Calcaveccia found to his cost at the Ryder Cup in 1991 – when *dormie-four* over Colin Montgomerie, he lost the last four holes, allowing the European to secure a vital half-point.

dot ball

[cricket] – *a delivery off which no runs are scored and no wicket is taken*

After this kind of ball, the scorer has nothing to write in the scorebook other than a *dot*, which is used to indicate that the ball has taken place but that there was nothing significant to record.

duck

[cricket] – *a score of zero by a batsman*

The term *making a duck's egg* originated in the 1860s to denote this unfortunate and quick outcome to a batsman's innings. It's thought to have started as a result of a spectator who, because a zero looks like a duck's egg, decided to quack at a disconsolate batsman as he returned to the pavilion. It's since been abbreviated to *duck* but has also gained several prefixes with varying meanings, including *golden, royal* and *diamond*.

Duckworth-Lewis method

[cricket] – *a mathematical system used to calculate revised target scores for the side batting second in a rain-affected one-day match*

This system takes its name from its statistician co-creators, Frank *Duckworth* and Tony *Lewis*. It was first used in 1997 and had taken over from its flawed predecessors by the 1999 World Cup. It's since been fully adopted by the International Cricket Council and is now the standard rain rule for first-class cricket across the world. Although the formula is apparently relatively simple to apply when needed, that doesn't mean I can explain how it works!

eagle

[golf] – *a score of two under par on a hole*

The term *eagle* began to be used by golfers in America in the 1920s as a development of the theme established by **birdie** earlier in the century. As the national symbol of the United States, the eagle was the obvious choice of bird, while it also represented the rarity and impressive nature of scoring two under **par** on a hole. It was adopted in Europe soon after and is now universally established across the golfing world.

Eau Rouge

[motor racing] – *the famous chicane at Spa-Francorchamps circuit in Belgium*

Widely considered one of the greatest corners on any racetrack in the world, *Eau Rouge* takes its name from a small stream that crosses the track at this point for the first time.

Eisenhower Tree

[golf] – *a 65-ft, 120-year-old loblolly pine tree on hole 17 at the Augusta National Course*

This is named after former US President and club member Dwight D. *Eisenhower* who, having hit his ball into it so many times, proposed at a club governors' meeting in 1956 that it should be cut down. So outraged was the club's chairman, Cliff Roberts, that he adjourned the meeting immediately, and the tree has been linked with Eisenhower ever since.

In spite of this, the club did build Eisenhower his own cabin on its grounds. It was built to Secret Service security specifications, some believed, solely to protect him from the chairman!

Eskimo roll

[canoeing] – *use of the body and paddle to right a canoe or kayak after capsizing without leaving the vessel*

Eskimos are thought to have been using kayaks for over 3,000 years and to have developed this move, which is named in their honour. They developed the roll in order to minimise time spent in the freezing waters that could kill within minutes. It was also essential that they didn't fall out of the kayak, as Eskimos are thought not have known how to swim.

flipper

[cricket] – *a faster delivery from a leg-spinner bowled with back-spin, causing it to skid off the pitch, fast and low*

This delivery was reputedly invented by the Australian Clarence Grimmett in the early part of the 20th century. He's thought to have developed and perfected it while bowling to a marked area in his backyard, using his dog to retrieve each delivery.

Once perfected, it helped him go on to become the first player to take 200 Test wickets. He bowled so many *flippers* that he prompted the great Don Bradman to suggest that he must have forgotten how to bowl his stock leg-break. In response, he bowled Bradman in a match a few days later with a leg-break.

Because of the action required by the hand to generate the flipper, it's common for the fingers to make a clicking sound as they release the ball – so in order to confuse the batsman while bowling leg-breaks, Grimmett would click the fingers on his left hand while releasing the ball from his right.

fore

[golf] – *a word shouted at anyone in danger of being hit by a ball*

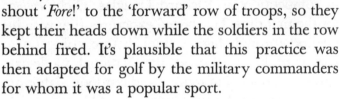

Although the definite origin of this exclamation is unknown, there are two different theories.

In the days of the British Redcoats lining up in rows to fire their muskets at the approaching enemy, the commander would shout '*Fore!*' to the 'forward' row of troops, so they kept their heads down while the soldiers in the row behind fired. It's plausible that this practice was then adapted for golf by the military commanders for whom it was a popular sport.

However, the more likely explanation comes from the practice of using two **caddies** in the 17th century; one to carry the golfer's clubs and the other, the *forecaddie*, to go on ahead to spot where the ball landed. If the player thought that the forecaddie was in danger, he would shout 'Fore!' to alert him to the approaching ball.

The standard of my golf means I use the expression a little too regularly!

Fosbury flop

[athletics] – *a method of high-jumping in which the athlete crosses the bar backwards with the body horizontal and the back facing the ground*

This technique was assigned its name by a journalist from Medford, Oregon, after being used in competition by Richard Douglas 'Dick' *Fosbury* for the first time. He started experimenting with his method through high school, before going on to win with it in 1968 at the National Collegiate Athletic Association indoor and outdoor high-jump titles while a student at Oregon State University. At the Summer Olympics in Mexico City later that year, it won him the ultimate prize – a gold medal and a new Olympic record of 2.24 metres.

furlong

[horse racing] – *a distance of one eighth of a mile*

For some time before the Norman Conquest in 1066, Saxon farmers in England had been using *furlongs* to measure distance. The word comes from the Old English *fuhrlang*, meaning *the length of a furrow*. It represented an eighth of a mile – theoretically, the ideal length for a field as it was the distance that a team of oxen could plough before needing a rest. Over time, this unit of distance was adopted by the horse-racing community.

Garryowen

[rugby union] – *a very high up-and-under kick*

The idea of this move is that, if high enough, it gives the kicker sufficient time to run forward and put all his colleagues back on side, which allows several of them to compete for the ball as it comes down. It takes its name from *Garryowen* Football Club in Limerick, Ireland; the rugby club that invented the tactic some time after it was founded in 1884.

The term has more recently been adopted by the game of football for teams that don't play the ball on the ground. It's usually applied to desperate teams that, through lack of strength in midfield, resort to hitting the long and high ball from the back to a lone striker.

Gaylord flip

[gymnastics] – *a move that comprises a one-and-a-half front salto over the high bar before grabbing the bar again*

This internationally recognised move takes its name from the American gymnast Mitch *Gaylord*, who first performed it in competition in 1978. Gaylord later led the US team to an Olympic gold medal in 1984 and was the first American in history to receive a perfect 10. Since retiring from the sport, he has appeared in  several Hollywood movies, including *Batman Forever* (1995), for which he had to draw on his gymnastics skills as Chris O'Donnell's stunt double in the role of Robin.

To this day, the *Gaylord flip* and the even more elaborate *Gaylord II* are still regarded as two of the most formidable and spectacular accomplishments in the sport.

Golden Bear

[golf] – *a nickname for the great Jack Nicklaus*

He acquired this moniker as a result of his golden yellow hair. However, earlier in his career – until he lost weight in his thirties and established the true extent of his brilliance as a golfer, and consequent respect and admiration from the public – he was often referred to as *Ohio Fats* or *Fat Jack*.

Outside my football heroes, the *Golden Bear* is my favourite sporting icon.

golden goal

[football] – *a goal scored in extra time that instantly decides the match winner*

This rule was introduced to encourage attacking football and ultimately reduce the number of penalty shoot-outs. Other sports use the term *sudden death* for this rule, but the Fédération Internationale de Football Association (FIFA) – upon introducing the new rule at the European Championship finals in 1996 – decided to call it the *golden goal*, as sudden death was deemed too negative. In 2002, the Union of European Football Associations (UEFA) introduced the *silver goal* as well, whereby the team leading after the first fifteen minutes of extra time would win. After the European Championship finals in Portugal in 2004, however, both were removed from the laws of the game. This is a shame in my view, as I still think that the golden goal is a better and fairer way of settling finals than a penalty shoot-out.

golf

[golf] – *a sport played outdoors with clubs and a ball over a course of usually eighteen, but sometimes nine, holes*

The word *golf* is thought to have derived linguistically from the Dutch word *kolf,* meaning *club*. Kolf was a game played by the Dutch with a stick and ball on Holland's frozen canals in the winter. It's thought that Kolf reached the east coast of Scotland with Dutch sailors in the 14th century as a result of the considerable shipping trade between the two countries at the time. The Scots then adopted it, relocating it to the public grassy **links** on the coast, and over time it developed into the game we know today.

The first written reference to golf was in the statutes of the Scottish Parliament in 1457, when James II banned the sport because it interfered with archery practice and military training (this ban lasted until 1502). A number of similar bans of popular sports were made by James II of Scotland and several other monarchs, during that era of particular unrest with France (see also **cricket**).

Golf was spelt in a number of ways at that time, including *goff, goif, gouff* and *gowf*, before the invention of dictionaries, people largely wrote words phonetically, and that was how the Scots pronounced it. Only later, by the 16th century, did 'golf' become the common spelling that is still used today.

There are still a number of people who maintain that golf is an acronym for *Gentlemen Only, Ladies Forbidden,* but while there are still golf clubs that don't allow women members, this theory is untrue.

googly

[cricket] – *an off-break bowled with an apparent leg-break action in an attempt to deceive the batsman*

This type of ball is occasionally referred to as a *bosie* or *bosey*, after its inventor Bernard Bosanquet. He first revealed it jokingly during breaks in matches to amuse his fellow players. In time, however, it became regarded as a serious part of a leg-bowler's arsenal, mystifying batsmen so much that it made their eyes 'goggle'. The press then coined the term *googly* while Bosanquet and England were on a tour of Australia and New Zealand in 1902.

Asked by many at the time whether his googly might be illegal, Bosanquet replied: 'No. Only immoral.' This is perhaps why in Australia, to this day, it's still referred to as a *wrong'un*.

Greco-Roman

[wrestling] – *a form of the sport in which only the upper body may be used for attacks*

This style of wrestling practised in Olympic and international amateur competition takes its name from its imitation of classical Greek and Roman representations of the sport. Thought to have originated with the ancient Greeks, it was then adapted and practised by soldiers throughout the Roman Empire 2,000 years ago.

Its most famous practitioner, Abraham Lincoln, was reputedly embroiled in a *Greco-Roman* bout when he was informed that he had been elected President of the United States in 1861.

Grand Prix

[motor racing] – *a type of race*

The first race to use this title was organised by the Automobile Club de France and run over two days at Le Mans in June 1906. It was won by the Hungarian-born Ferencz Szisz, who covered the 700 miles in a Renault at an average speed of 63 mph. Although today the term is most commonly associated with Formula One, it was initially used to describe the principal race in a region, whatever class of car it may have been – the drivers were contesting the *Grand* or *Big Prize*. After the end of the First World War, interest in motor sport grew rapidly. A series of *Grand Prix* races across Europe were reserved exclusively for Formula One before an annual Grand Prix calendar was put in place.

Grand Slam

[golf and tennis] – *the winning of all four major championships in the same year*

This term is borrowed from baseball, in which it denotes a home run hit when the team has a runner at each base and as a result scores four runs. There's a kind of reverse logic in that one swing of the bat with the bases loaded can achieve four runs, whereas in tennis and golf, a player has to win four tournaments in order to achieve the *Grand Slam*.

The term was first used for tennis in 1933 by American journalist John Kieran when describing the attempt that year by Australian Jack Crawford to win what have since become the four Grand Slam tournaments (the Australian Open, French Open, US Open and Wimbledon).

The expression was later adopted fully by the

golfing world, although someone is yet to win it with the current set of Majors (Masters, Open Championship, US Open and US PGA). Tiger Woods has come closest by holding all four simultaneously, only not in the same calendar year. This achievement has since been referred to as a *Consecutive Grand Slam* or a *Tiger Slam*. In tennis, it's possible to win the *Golden Slam* by winning the four Grand Slam tournaments as well as the gold medal for tennis at the Summer Olympics. This feat has been achieved only once – by Steffi Graf, in 1988.

The term has been taken up by a number of other sports over the years, including rugby union's Six Nations Championship, in which a team must win all of its five matches to secure the Grand Slam. However, rugby adopted the expression in the days of the Five Nations Championship, when only four wins were needed, making it true to its baseball origins.

Green Jacket

[golf] – *jacket worn by members of Augusta National Golf Club and awarded to winners of the Masters, which is played there*

This single-breasted jacket is coloured what is known as *Masters green*, and adorned with gold buttons and the club logo. It was introduced in 1937 and worn by club members during the **Masters** so that spectators could identify a reliable source of information. Although this practice continued, it was 1949 before what is now one of the most prized possessions in golf was awarded for the first time – the recipient was Sam Snead, the tournament champion for that year.

gully

[cricket] – *a fielding position on the off-side, almost square to the batsman at the end of a slip cordon*

It's thought that Arthur Owen Jones invented this position in the 1880s while still at school, before he went on to play for and then captain England. Its name comes from the word *gully* in its everyday sense, suggestive of the channel left between the slips and the point before a player was positioned there.

As it's principally a catching position, another suggestion is that the term comes from the 16th-century word *gull* meaning *gullet* or *throat*, whereby a player fielding there should *swallow* the ball when it comes to them.

Gunners

[football] – *the nickname for Arsenal FC*

In late 1886, a group of workers at the Royal Arsenal Armament Factory in Woolwich decided to form a football team. They called it *Dial Square* after a section of the workshops in the middle of the factory, and played their first match on 11 December of the same year, beating Eastern Wanderers 6-0. A few weeks later, they renamed themselves *Royal Arsenal,* and in 1888 adopted their first crest. The design was based predominantly on the coat of arms for the Borough of Woolwich and comprised three columns, which, although looking like chimneys, were in fact cannons.

After a few years of playing friendlies and entering local cup competitions, 1891 saw them become the first London club to turn professional – at the same time, changing their name to *Woolwich Arsenal.* In 1893, they also became the first London club to be admitted to the Football League. Starting off in the Second Division, they won promotion to the First in 1904. Despite this, their location meant lower attendances than other clubs, and so before long the club was in financial difficulty. In 1910, Fulham chairman Henry Norris took over Woolwich Arsenal with the intention of merging the two clubs. The Football League vetoed the idea, however, so Norris looked to relocate Woolwich Arsenal elsewhere. Initially sites in Battersea and Harringay were considered, before he finally chose the playing fields of St John's College of Divinity in Highbury. With the move, the Woolwich prefix was dropped and so the club became simply *Arsenal FC*.

In 1922, in the first match-day programme of the season, the club revealed a new crest; an east-pointing single cannon accompanied by the inscription, *The Gunners*. The design was amended again in 1925 to a slimmer and westward-facing cannon, but the inscription remained. Although the cannon then went largely unchanged until 2002, when it was pointed back east, the inscription had disappeared by 1949 – it was no longer required. Gunners had become the nickname for what is, without question, the greatest football club in the world!

haka

[rugby union] – *a traditional Maori war dance performed by the All Blacks before the start of a match*

According to Maori mythology, Tane-rore, the child of the Sun God and the Summer maid, created the *haka* that was then performed in different forms by warriors before going into battle. 'Haka' is the general term for Maori dance, and a version of this, the *Ka mate*, was first performed by the **All Blacks** in 1905. A hundred years later, at a Tri Nations match against South Africa in 2005, they unexpectedly introduced a new and much more aggressive haka called *Kapa o Pango*, which concludes with an ominous throat-slitting action directed at the opposing team. It will not act as a replacement for *Ka mate*, but instead will be reserved for 'special occasions'. I think it remains the most spectacular and intimidating piece of psychological warfare within the sporting arena.

hand of God

[football] – *the name given by Diego Maradona to his infamous hand-ball in 1990*

Four years after the Falklands War, Argentina and England met in the 1986 World Cup quarter-finals. Animosity was rife, with some fighting among the 114,580 fans in Mexico City's Aztec Stadium. Six minutes into the second half with the score still 0-0, Maradona played a one-two with team-mate Jorge Valdano on the edge of the box. England's Steve Hodge intercepted the ball but failed to clear it, accidentally looping it up towards goalkeeper Peter Shilton and into the path of the advancing Maradona. Now it doesn't take a genius to work out that at 6'1'', Shilton should be able to punch the ball comfortably clear over a 5'6'' Maradona trying to head it. Instead Maradona,

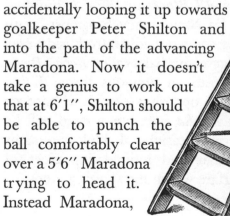

by using his hand, beat Shilton in the challenge, scoring a goal and giving Argentina a 1-0 lead.

Covering the World Cup for BBC TV, I had an initial struggle to convince my colleagues that Maradona had used his hand. I was accused of supporting Peter Shilton, by being a member of the goalkeepers' union. We were watching it in a studio on the top floor but quickly ran downstairs to the videotape room in the basement, where the replay soon came to my rescue.

At the post-match press conference, Maradona claimed that the goal was scored 'a little bit by the *hand of God*, another bit by the head of Maradona'. For quite some time, the English press referred to it as the 'hand of the Devil'. More recently, in his 2002 autobiography, Maradona wrote, 'At the time I called it "the hand of God"', going on to admit proudly that this was nonsense, as 'it was the hand of Diego! And it felt a little bit like pickpocketing the English.'

hat-trick

[cricket] – *the feat of taking three wickets with consecutive balls*

Although this term has now spread to other sports (notably football, for which it denotes that a player has scored three goals in a single match), its origin is in the game of **cricket**. In 1858 during a match at the Hyde Park ground in Sheffield, the bowler H.H. Stephenson – playing for an All-England XI – took three wickets with consecutive balls. It was customary at the time to reward outstanding sporting feats, so a collection was taken and used to buy a hat for Stephenson.

In time, this practice and expression made its way across the Atlantic to 1940s Toronto, where a haberdasher would award a free hat to any Maple Leaf ice-hockey player who scored three goals in a game. This in turn led to the tradition still seen today at North American ice-hockey games, whereby fans shower the ice with their hats when a player scores a *hat-trick*.

haymaker

[boxing] – *an unrestrained punch usually leading to a knockout, whereby the fist is swung wide in an arc*

In the days of producing hay by hand, the worker or *haymaker* would slice at the grass with large swings of a scythe, causing it to fall to the ground in a heap. The term is thought to have entered the boxing lexicon at the beginning of the 20th century.

Hell Bunker

[golf] – *718 square yards of sand on the 14th hole on the Old Course, St Andrews*

As the largest bunker on the course and at over 10 feet deep, its name speaks for itself. And similarly to Hell, once you are in it, it's extremely difficult to get out of – as the mighty Jack Nicklaus (or the **Golden Bear**) found to his cost at the 1995 Open, when he took four strokes to do so, scoring a 10 for the hole.

hockey

[hockey] – *a sport played with sticks, a ball and two goals by two teams of eleven players*

Although historical records indicate that *hockey* has been played in some form or other for over 4,000 years, it was not until the mid-1800s that it acquired its current name. At this time, a Colonel named John Hockey, while stationed at the garrison on Fort Edward, Nova Scotia, used a game very similar to the one we know today as a way of keeping his soldiers conditioned. These workouts soon came to be known as playing *Hockey's game*.

jockey

[horse racing] – *a person who rides horses in races as a profession*

The word *jockey* is thought to have surfaced around the end of the 15th century, as an extension of the Scottish name *Jock* which was, and still is, a generic Scottish term for a man or boy. In the following century, 'jockey' began to be used to describe men of an untrustworthy nature, and in time, the verb *to jockey* came to mean *to outsmart* or *to get the better of*. Although this propensity to trick or cheat didn't necessarily apply to racers of horses at the time, their job was principally to manoeuvre their horse into an advantageous position within a racing pack by any means necessary, and perhaps some early jockeys employed underhand tactics to do so.

Apprentice jockeys always have an asterisk after their name in an official race programme to denote them as such. Because of the symbol's supposed resemblance to a bug, apprentice jockeys are known as *bug boys*.

King of the Mountains

[cycling] – *the leader on points accumulated in the mountain stages of the Tour de France*

In the Tour de France, points are awarded for the first rider over the top of each mountain. Every climb through the Alps and Pyrenees is rated for difficulty, from the easiest, *Category Four*, through to *Hors Catégorie*, which means *outside category* – so unpleasant it's beyond classification! The rider with the most points gained through this section of the race is recognised as *King of the Mountains*. This esteemed classification was first recognised in 1933 and won by Spaniard Vicente Trueba. The winner is sometimes also affectionately referred to as the *Mountain Goat* for his ability to climb.

In 1975, Tour organisers introduced and awarded the *polka-dot jersey* to the King of the Mountains in order to distinguish him from other riders. The design was based on the polka-dot wrapping of Poulain chocolate bars, the sponsors of the race at that time. During their tenure through the 1970s and 80s, the confectioner awarded each winner their own weight in chocolate!

lanterne rouge

[cycling] – *the overall last-place rider in a stage race*

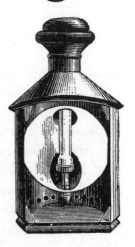

This is French for *red light*, alluding to the one found on the back of a train. In more prestigious races such as the Tour de France, the label of *lanterne rouge* carries more kudos and considerably more publicity and, as a consequence, more money-making potential than the rider who comes second from last. As a result, some riders in the past have been suspected of engineering themselves into last place in the closing stages of the race.

lacrosse

[lacrosse] – *a sport played with a ball, long-handled sticks with a webbed pouch on one end, and two goals, by two teams of ten players each*

Originally, around the end of the 15th century, the game was developed by North American indigenous peoples, as a way of training for war. They called it *baggataway* and played it on a huge pitch half a kilometre long. It was violent and, although there were few fixed rules, each tribe made a point of having their own slight variation. The Cherokee tribe played it with hundreds of people on each side and, true to its initially intended purpose, knew it as the *Little Brother of War*. It was later adopted as a sport and given its modern name by French settlers in the area. *La crosse* is French for a *bishop's crozier*, which is what the sticks used in the game resembled.

links

[golf] – *a course on low-lying ground on the coast*

Coming from the Anglo-Saxon word, *hlinc*, meaning *ridge*, this has come to mean a rough grassy area that links the land and sea. True links courses are therefore those by the sea where the soil is sandy and where the grass has short blades but long roots. Scotland has many such areas, which are useless for agriculture but ideal for golf (especially in winter) because drainage is good. They were also away from towns and villages, meaning that, when golf was banned by James II from 1457 to 1502, people could still play without any prying eyes seeing them. The same applied when play on the Sabbath was banned from 1580 to 1724.

Lions

[rugby union] – *a touring side comprising players from the British Isles*

Lions rugby began in 1888, when sporting entrepreneurs Arthur Shrewsbury and Alfred Shaw, having already taken an English cricket side on a tour of Australia, decided to move on to rugby. Although they successfully took a team of British and Irish players to Australia in 1888, the first official tour – whereby a committee from all four Home Unions picked the squad – was for a South Africa tour in 1910, by which time they were called the British Isles Rugby Union Team. This name remained until the tour of 1924, again to South Africa. They set out with their somewhat cumbersome title intact, but returned as the Lions – the new moniker chosen by the players because of the lion standing proudly above the crest on their official ties.

Little Master

[cricket] – *a nickname for Indian legend, Sunil Gavaskar*

Sunil Gavaskar is arguably the best opening batsman of all time. He gained the affectionate title of the *Little Master* due to his 5′4″ height and his phenomenal powers of concentration while demonstrating almost flawless technique. He scored 34 Test centuries in his career and was the first player to score more than 10,000 Test runs.

local derby

[football] – *a fixture between rivals from the same district*

Although this term is most commonly used for football, it can be applied to any sport. It's thought to have originated with a tradition started in the Elizabethan era in the town of Ashbourne in *Derbyshire*, a few miles from where I was born in Chesterfield. Each year, on Shrove Tuesday and Ash Wednesday, the people of the town board up shop windows and take to the streets to play the largest football match in the world. Although it is called the Ashbourne Royal Shrovetide Football Match, a fairly brutal game of rugby with fewer rules and a round ball might be a more accurate description. One team is made up of those born on the north side of the Henmore River, otherwise known as the Up'ards, and the other of those born on the south side – the Down'ards. The game kicks off at 2 pm and is then played until 10 pm on a pitch three miles long. As if that wasn't enough,

much of it is played out in the
cold waters of the Henmore,
including the two goals, which
were originally the wheels at
the two local mills.

In my twelve years at
Arsenal, there were rarely
more important, competitive
or violent encounters than our
local derbies with Spurs, our
North London rivals. Victory
for one or the other was hugely
important for both players and,
of course, the fans, in what is
always referred to as the *North London derby*.

Lord's

[cricket] – *the Test cricket ground and home of the Marylebone Cricket Club in St John's Wood, London*

In the first half of the 18th century, the nobility played their cricket in Islington's White Conduit Fields, but as London's population grew, so did the players' impatience with the large crowds that appeared to watch. Looking to move elsewhere, they asked *Thomas Lord*, a bowler with White Conduit Cricket Club and an ambitious entrepreneur of the time, if he would be interested in setting up a new ground. Lord duly leased a ground on Dorset Fields in Marylebone, where he staged his first match on 31 May 1787 – and so the *Marylebone Cricket Club* (MCC) was born. A year later, the club produced a set of laws for the game, and to this day remains cricket's governing authority around the world.

MCC then moved to Marylebone Bank in Regent's Park for a short period between 1811 and 1814, before moving to a new rural ground in St John's Wood that previously had been the site of a simple country duck pond. This is still, however, the site on which *Lord's* cricket ground – the spiritual home of cricket – stands to this day.

Louisville Lip

[boxing] – *a nickname for the great Muhammad Ali from his fighting days*

Cassius Marcellus Clay Jr. was born on 17 January 1942 in Louisville, Kentucky, and went on to become, in many people's opinion, the greatest heavyweight boxer the world has ever seen. Part of his armoury – accompanying his phenomenal physical power and speed in the *ring* – was an ability to unsettle other boxers through talk. He was a master at getting into an adversary's head, often overtly and accurately predicting the round in which he would knock his opponent out. Here are a few examples that helped earn him the nicknames *The Mouth* and the *Louisville Lip*:

> *'Frazier is so ugly that he should donate his face to the US Bureau of Wild Life.'*

'I'll beat him so bad he'll need a shoehorn to put his hat on.'

'It's hard to be humble when you're as great as I am.'

'I am the greatest, I said that even before I knew I was.'

As well as this slightly disparaging nickname, he was and still is more commonly known as *The Greatest*.

I am three months older than Ali and our sporting heights more or less ran parallel, albeit mine on a lesser stage than the great boxer. When he fought Sir Henry Cooper for the second time, the bout was staged at Highbury, home of Arsenal, and Clay used our dressing room to prepare.

love

[tennis] – *no score*

Reputedly this comes from the 18th-century expression *to play for love of the game*, in which *love* acts as a substitute for *nothing*. Some also believe that it derives from the French word *l'oeuf* meaning *egg*, as the shape of the egg resembles the zero that the player has to their name.

madhouse

[darts] – *double one*

This name is born out of the frustration felt by many players in the past, as they struggle to finish the game with their least favourite and most difficult double. Also, by finding yourself on a score of two, the only way that remains to finish the game is by hitting a double one and so, until you've done it, you are confined to the *madhouse*.

Madison

[cycling] – *a 50-km track race, with two teams of two riders competing for points during intermittent sprints*

This race is slightly peculiar in that, although all four riders go round the track simultaneously, only one rider from each team can compete at any one time. While one is involved in a sprint, their teammate conserves energy by circling the top of the banked track before being propelled back into action by grabbing the sprinter's hand. This is known as a *handsling*.

The race takes its name from *Madison Square Garden* in New York City, where it was first contested in the 1930s.

maiden

[cricket] – *an over in which no runs were scored*

Although now considered old-fashioned in an everyday context, the word *maiden* was used to describe a young unmarried girl, who was consequently almost certainly a virgin. In other words, a *maiden over* is one that the batsman has not managed to deflower.

mankad

[cricket] – *a form of dismissal whereby the bowler removes the bails instead of bowling if the batsman at the non-striker's end backs up too far*

This type of run-out takes its name from Mulvantrai 'Vinoo' *Mankad*, one of the greatest all-rounders India has ever produced. He caused controversy on India's 1947–48 cricket tour of Australia by removing opening batsman Bill Brown in this fashion at the Sydney Cricket Ground (SCG) in the second Test. It was not the first time he had dismissed Brown in this way on the tour either; it happened in an earlier match against an Australian XI at the same ground, but on that occasion he warned Brown before running him out.

The Australian press were unforgiving, labelling Mankad's actions as outrageous and unsportsmanlike. However, some Australians saw it differently – including the great Don Bradman, who later defended Mankad in his autobiography:

For the life of me I can't understand why the press questioned his sportsmanship. The laws of cricket make it quite clear that the non-striker must keep within his ground until the ball has been delivered. If not, why is the provision there which enables the bowler to run him out? By backing up too far or too early the non-striker is very obviously gaining an unfair advantage.

Some people even considered the warning that Mankad had given Brown before getting him out as one of the most sporting acts the SCG had ever seen.

So, whichever side of the fence you sit on with regards to the morality of Mankad's actions, if you are run out in this fashion, then you are the victim of a *mankad* or have been *mankaded.*

marathon

[athletics] – *a 26-mile, 385-yard race*

In 490 BC, the Ionian Greeks attacked and destroyed the Persian colony of Sardis. Persia responded immediately by invading Greece, where the considerably more substantial and  better-equipped Persian army were met by the Greeks on the plains of *Marathon*. Despite the disparity in numbers and weaponry, the Greeks were victorious. The legend has it that Pheidippides, the best runner in Greece, then ran the 26 miles from Marathon to Athens and, upon announcing the good news, died on the spot from exhaustion.

At the birth of the modern Olympic Games in Athens in 1896, a long-distance run was incorporated that covered the route of 26 miles and 385 yards chosen by Pheidippides from the Battle of Marathon over two millennia before.

mashie niblick

[golf] – *a century-old hickory-shafted club with a loft between a mashie and a niblick, similar to a modern 9-iron, only with a longer shaft*

The name for a *mashie* is thought to have come from the Old Scottish word *mash*, which was used in the past as another name for a sledgehammer. The link with the sledgehammer is in the action involved. With a *massé* in **snooker**, the cue is brought down in a sharp stab from above so as to impart spin to the ball, and there is a similar theory in how to get the most out of a mashie.

A *niblick* is another old-fashioned, deep-bladed club for lofted shots particularly from the sand and deep rough. The name is thought to have come from *nib*, which refers to the *nose* (or *toe* as it is now more commonly known) being shorter than on any other wooden-shafted club of the time.

Although now fairly obsolete, the mashie, the niblick and the composite club, the deep-grooved or dimple-faced *mashie niblick*, were once a popular inclusion in a lot of golf bags: 'If your ball is lying in an almost unplayable position, try one of these mashie niblicks!' exclaimed the Army & Navy catalogue of 1907. It was certainly my Scottish dad's favourite golf club, as by his own admission it was constantly getting him out of trouble!

Masters

[golf] – *tournament played every spring at the Augusta National Golf Club*

In 1934, Bobby Jones and Clifford Roberts, co-founders of the club, organised the inaugural Augusta National Invitation Tournament. Roberts had wanted to call it the *Masters* but Jones objected, thinking it too presumptuous. It kept its initial name for another five years, until Jones eventually relented and it officially became the Masters in 1939.

Michelle

[cricket] – *a five-wicket haul by a bowler in a single innings*

This is rhyming slang for the word *fifer*, a cricketer's contraction of the term *five-for*. It takes its name from the American Hollywood actress *Michelle* Pfeiffer.

Milky Bar Kid

[darts] – *a nickname for former World Champion, Keith Deller*

In 1983, Keith Deller became the first and still youngest ever qualifier to be crowned World Champion. On his way to the final he beat third seed John Lowe and then second seed Jocky Wilson, before meeting top seed Eric Bristow in the final. 'He's not just an underdog', said the commentator Sid Waddell of 23-year-old Deller: 'He's the underpuppy.' Needless to say, he won the final. He acquired his nickname from the character used to advertise chocolate bars throughout the 1980s – as a result of his age and his clean-cut image, and because he drank milk during his games.

mulligan

[golf] – *a free extra shot sometimes taken as a second chance in a social match*

There are several different stories that circulate as a possible origin of this word, three of which cite a Canadian golfer, David *Mulligan*. Mulligan was a successful hotelier of the time and played much of his golf at St Lambert in Montreal during the 1920s. The first story suggests that on one occasion, having hit a very long drive off the tee but not in the right direction, he placed another ball on the tee and hit that as well, explaining it to his friends as a 'correction shot'. They were amused by his behaviour but felt it deserved a better name and so called it a mulligan.

The second story tells of Mulligan's friends allowing him a free shot as a result of him having to drive them along the bumpy and windy road to the club that morning.

The third version is that he overslept and having rushed frantically to make it to the first tee in time, hit an awful drive, and so his friends let him have another.

Some also believe – although it seems unlikely as it occurred later than the other stories – that it takes its name from a John A. 'Buddy' Mulligan, a locker-room attendant at Essex Fells, New Jersey, in the 1930s. John Mulligan was well known for his propensity to replay shots, particularly on the first tee. Whichever story you believe, the term had gained widespread use on golf courses by the 1940s.

Nelson

[cricket] – *the score of 111 or multiples thereof, considered unlucky by many cricketers*

111 is considered unlucky due to its resemblance to the three **stumps** with the **bails** missing. The name was coined thanks to the common misconception that Admiral Horatio *Nelson* had lost one arm, one eye and one leg in battle, whereas he had the use of both of his legs until his death at the Battle of Trafalgar in 1805.

There is an old superstition that originates from Gloucestershire, whereby to avoid being out while on Nelson, the whole team except the batsmen must keep their feet off the ground. Before his retirement in 2005, the great umpire David Shepherd could always be seen giving a hop on one foot until the score changed.

222 is known as *double Nelson*, 333 as *triple Nelson* and so on. The Australian equivalent of Nelson is the **devil's number**. This is any score that includes 87, which is thought to be bad luck as it's 13 short of a century.

nightwatchman

[cricket] – *a lower-order batsman sent in as an alternative to the scheduled, more skilled batsman, towards the close of play*

Some believe this to be an illogical practice – for example, Steve Waugh never employed the tactic in his tenure as Australian captain. But the rationale is that sending in a top-order batsman late in the day places them in a no-win situation; they can't achieve a great deal in the short time available, and if their wicket falls, it will have an even more detrimental effect on the team. Therefore, the lower-order batsman is sent in with the sole purpose of surviving until the end of the day so that he remains in overnight, returning with everything safely in place in the morning – hence his title, the *nightwatchman*.

Although the nightwatchman is called upon to play a predominantly defensive role, and as a result very little is expected of them in terms of runs, there have been a few notable exceptions to this. In 1988, England wicketkeeper Jack Russell was sent in as a nightwatchman on his Test debut against Sri Lanka at **Lord's**, but went on to score 94 – his then highest first-class score. Harold Larwood, when sent in at number four instead of his customary number nine against Australia in the **Bodyline** Series of 1932–33, scored 98. More recently, Alex Tudor, while playing for England against New Zealand and without a first-class century to his name, was sent in as nightwatchman with England needing 210 to win. He guided England to victory, remaining unbeaten on 99. In April 2006, Jason Gillespie surpassed the previous record of 105 set by fellow-Australian Anthony Mann against India in 1977, by making 201 not out against Bangladesh.

Nine Dart

[darts] – *a nickname for British Darts Organisation stalwart Shaun Greatbatch*

Nine is the fewest number of darts that a player can possibly throw to win a game of 501. It's the ultimate *checkout* (finish to a game) and notoriously difficult to achieve. In 1984, John Lowe became the first player to have a televised nine-dart finish, but it was in fact recorded from a game earlier in the day. At the Dutch Open in 2002, Shaun Greatbatch became the first player ever to do it live on television, subsequently earning him the nickname *Nine Dart*.

nineteenth hole

[golf] – *the clubhouse bar*

So called because it's usually the next destination for players after the 18th green. Although references to this term are evident from the very beginning of the 20th century, it's thought to have later been assigned a permanent place in the golfing lexicon by the work of P.G. Wodehouse, many of whose short stories were told through a fictional character on the terrace of the *nineteenth hole.*

nutmeg

[football] – *a skilful move in which a player deliberately passes the ball through his opponent's legs and retrieves it on the other side*

A term that is thought to have been inspired by deceitful practice in the *nutmeg* trade during the Victorian era, whereby American exporters would cut their batches of nutmeg with similar looking bits of wood. The recipients deceived, or *nutmegged* as it came to be known, were left looking foolish, as is the victim of a nutmeg on a football field. In the current game, players affectionately use the term *nuts* when a team-mate or an opponent is on the receiving end of this skill.

oche

[darts] – *the line behind which a player has to stand when throwing darts*

This word was officially recognised by the British Darts Organisation only in the late 1970s. From the 1920s, the word *hockey* was used instead. Although the reason is unclear, it's thought that this came about because people used the crates from a West Country brewery called *Hockey and Sons* to  standardise the distance between the player and the board. The crates were two feet in length, so pubs used four of them to mark out the eight feet that was the standard distance for many years, and in some places, still is.

Over time, the *h* was dropped, so phonetically it became *ockey* and then acquired the new spelling, *oche*.

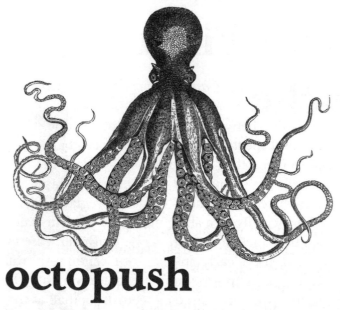

octopush

[octopush] – *a type of underwater hockey played in a 25-metre swimming pool with a lead puck, by two teams of ten – only six of whom are allowed in the water at any one time*

This game was invented by a group of subaqua divers in Southsea, England, at the end of the summer in 1954, in order to spice up the winter confined to diving in their local swimming pool. It soon spread to the United States, South Africa and Australasia.

According to its inventors, the rules of the sport were determined by the word *octopus*: originally it was to be played with teams of eight (*octo*) wielding sticks which they used to *push* the puck (or *squid*).

Old Firm

[football] – *Celtic and Rangers Football Clubs*

The rivalry between these two clubs is one of the oldest and most ferocious in world football, going back to when they first met at Celtic Park in 1888, watched by around 2,000 fans. Today, this collective term for these two Glaswegian clubs is used principally as a short nickname – for instance, when they meet in a ***local derby***. However, when it was first used early in the 20th century, it was intended as a more scathing implication that the two clubs were in charge of Scottish football at that time, and ran it without consideration of other clubs. The term was chosen to signify the lucrative aspect of their frequent meetings, and the belief that the two clubs colluded to ensure their own profit and consequent domination, at the expense of the other Scottish clubs.

Whether this is true or not, no two teams across the world have dominated their national championship like Celtic and Rangers. As of 2006, between them they have won 91 of the 109 Scottish titles available since 1890.

Although I never knew him, a great uncle of mine – Sir John Ure Primrose – was Chairman of Rangers at the turn of the 20th century, and in 1902 he officially opened Hampden Park.

on the hoof

[rugby union] – *a player in action*

This phrase can only really be said properly by one man: its inventor and chief exponent – the great Bill McLaren. Before his illustrious career in commentating, which lasted more than 50 years, he was on the verge of playing for Scotland at flanker, when he contracted a form of tuberculosis that almost killed him. Needless to say, it brought his playing career to a premature end, but although the game lost out in one area, it gained immeasurably in another. While recovering from his illness, he began to commentate on table-tennis matches on the hospital radio, before going on to be the greatest commentator of rugby union the world has ever known. Although now retired, to the extreme detriment of the game, he will always be remembered for an endless number of catchphrases, not least of all: 'Seventeen stones of Scottish prop *on the hoof*!' A wonderful man and a former BBC colleague – in short, a national treasure.

on the rivet

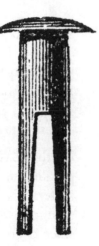

[cycling] – *to ride as fast as possible*

On old leather types of saddle, a copper rivet was used at the front to hold the leather in place. When riders are at their physical limit, they naturally sit nearer the front of the saddle and so are said to be *on the rivet*.

outjump the hill

[ski-jumping] – *to jump beyond the point where the landing area ends and the hill flattens out, otherwise known as the k point, or critical point*

In the past, ski-jumpers always kept their skis parallel in flight. In 1985, Sweden's Jan Boklöv suffered a mild epileptic attack while mid-jump, seizing his body and skis in the V position that has since been adopted by all professional practitioners of the sport across the world. This technique enabled jumpers to fly beyond the *k point* for the first time, and so Boklöv inadvertently made it possible to *outjump the hill*.

out of the screws

[golf] – *a big drive*

This expression goes back to the days when wooden drivers had four wood screws surrounding the middle of the clubface. If the ball came *out of the screws*, it meant that it came out of the *sweet spot* and so the shot invariably went a long way.

Oval

[cricket] – *a Test cricket ground in Kennington, London*

The *Oval* came about in the 1790s, when an oval road was built around what was then a cabbage patch. Subsequently, the land was turned into a market garden but was later closed through lack of interest. It became a sports ground in 1845 after 10,000 grass turfs were brought in from Tooting Common at a cost of £300. It staged the first FA Cup Final in 1872, the first England football international in 1873, the first England vs. Wales and England vs. Scotland rugby internationals in 1876, the first cricket Test on English soil in 1880, and the inaugural Ashes Test in 1882. Owned by the Prince of Wales, it certainly was and still is one of the most important sports grounds in the world.

pair of spectacles

[cricket] – *two ducks in the same match*

If a batsman has two zeros to his name in a game, they are said to resemble the lenses of a *pair of spectacles*. If a player loses his wicket on the first ball of each innings, then he has two *golden **ducks*** to his name – which constitute a *king pair*.

Palooka

[boxing] – *an inexperienced or incompetent boxer*

In 1930 American Ham Fisher started *Joe Palooka*, which ran until 1984, turning out to be one of the most successful comic strips of all time. Although the eponymous Palooka was a patriotic, likeable and morally sound heavyweight championship boxer of the highest quality, he wasn't particularly bright and so, over time, his name was somewhat unfairly adopted by the boxing community to represent an inexperienced or incompetent boxer.

par

[golf] – *the benchmark score for quality play on a specific hole or course*

Some believe that *par* is an acronym of *professional average result* – although given the word's history this seems unlikely. It was originally used on the stock exchange, where a stock may be above or below its normal or par price. It was used in a golfing context for the first time in 1870, when golf writer A.H. Doleman asked James Anderson and David Strath, two competitors for the Open Championship at Prestwick, what score would win it. They thought that 49 would be sufficient on Prestwick's twelve holes, which Doleman subsequently labelled as par. The tournament was then won by Young Tom Morris with a score of two over par.

In time, different governing bodies across the golfing world standardised par to represent the score which all golfers should try to equal, if not better.

Pigeon

[cricket] – *a nickname for Glenn McGrath*

Glenn Donald McGrath is one of the most highly regarded bowlers in the history of the game and has played an essential role in Australia's domination of world cricket for over ten years. He's taken more Test wickets than any other fast bowler who has ever graced a cricket pitch. Needless to say, this doesn't grant him immunity from the nickname of *Pigeon*, which he acquired from team-mate Brad McNamara while playing for New South Wales. 'You've stolen a pigeon's legs, McGrath!' exclaimed McNamara upon seeing his spindly pins in the dressing room.

pits

[motor racing] – *the area next to the track where teams service the cars*

Motor racing began almost immediately after the successful construction of the first petrol-fuelled cars, with the inaugural Paris to Rouen race in 1894. The following year saw the formation of the first motor racing club and America also held its first race. As the sport grew, racing cars developed and as the speeds increased, so did the need for greater maintenance – take the winning Mercedes in the French Grand Prix in 1908, for example, which shredded ten tyres on its way to victory! So in the same year, the Targa Florio – an open road endurance race held near Palermo in Sicily – saw the introduction of *pits*. These were shallow trenches dug next to the track to allow the mechanics to replace the detachable tyre rims in use at the time.

Pits have developed significantly since then and, among the banks of monitors and computer equipment, regularly see pit crews refuel a car and change all four wheels in less than seven seconds!

pole position

[motor racing] – *the number one slot on the starting grid*

Pole position is the optimal place to start a race from. Not only is it nearer the start line than any other car, it's also positioned so that the driver can take the first corner on the inside, and consequently shorter, line of the track. The term comes from horse-racing in the mid-19th century, when, if a horse 'had the pole', it had drawn the starting position nearest the post that denoted the starting line, on the inside boundary rails. It was adopted by the motor racing community in the 1950s.

pool

[pool] – *a form of billiards played with balls and a cue on a baize-covered table with six pockets*

Billiards, originally played with three balls, was principally a two-player contest until the beginning of the 19th century. At this time, the British added more balls and created two other types of game to allow room for more players. *Pyramids* was played with fifteen unnumbered red balls. Another multi-player game used a variable number of coloured and spotted balls in a form of ante betting that gave it its name of *pool*. Each player would put in a stake and the winner of the game would scoop the pool of cash. The game is thought to have gained its name in Britain by 1820, and reached France by 1923, when rules posters for *jeu de la poule* began to appear.

popping crease

[cricket] – *a line at each end of the pitch which a batsman must be behind to avoid being stumped or run out, and which a bowler must not overstep to avoid a no-ball being called*

The use of the term *crease* in cricket is in line with its basic meaning of *furrow*, two of which were originally cut in the pitch to mark out the necessary areas. This method was used until the introduction of painted white lines towards the end of the 19th century. The name *popping crease* comes from the very early days of the game. Before **stumps** (or their earlier predecessors) were introduced, there was a *popping hole* – a hole dug out of the pitch where the stumps now stand. Batsmen had to *pop* their bat in the hole on completion of a run and similarly, fielders had to *pop* the ball in it in order to run a batsman out (being bowled was not yet part of the game).

Postage Stamp

[golf] – *the 129-yard, par-3 8th hole at Royal Troon*

Originally this hole was called *Ailsa*, after Ailsa Craig, the prominent rock that emerges from the Atlantic off the Ayrshire coast and is clearly visible from the elevated tee. Although the shortest hole on any of the Open courses, it's far from the easiest, due to the tiny size of its green. In 1909, Willie Park Jr., a former Open Champion, described it in an article for *Golf Illustrated* as 'a pitching surface skimmed down to the size of a *postage stamp*', and the name stuck.

Because the green is surrounded by bunkers, the ball must reach it with the tee-shot. Tiger Woods found this out to his cost when he failed to find the green in the final round of the 1997 Open – shooting a triple-***bogey*** six as a result. At the Open in 1950, German Hermann Tissies took 15.

There have been successes there, of course, notably the hole-in-one by 71-year-old Gene Sarazen at the 1973 Open, 50 years after his appearance at Troon's inaugural Open in 1923. Despite this, it's still regarded by many as 'the hardest stamp in the world to lick'.

Pumas

[rugby union] – *the nickname of Argentina's national team*

When the side set off for South Africa in 1965, embarking on their first overseas tour, they were still without a nickname to rival the existing *Springboks* of their hosts. A reporter, trying to think of something suitable while following the tour, mistakenly took the jaguar on their team crest for a puma, and gave them the wrong name. Undeterred by the error, the press and the public continued to use the name before the team itself eventually adopted it. The crest of the *Pumas* still depicts a jaguar today.

pyjama cricket

[cricket] – *one-day cricket*

In 1977, Australian media mogul Kerry Packer and his Channel Nine network failed to win the television rights to cover Test matches and domestic cricket from the Australian Cricket Board. As a result, he set up a rival *World Series* by luring a number of high-profile players with very lucrative contracts. In order to also attract the necessary spectators, Packer introduced a number of innovations for the sport, such as night games with floodlights, coloured clothing, a white ball and black sightscreens. These concepts are still in use today for one-day cricket across the world, including the brightly-coloured team kits that give it the name *pyjama cricket*. The term is most commonly used in a derogatory context by purists of Test cricket who also sometimes refer to it as *hit and giggle*.

Queensberry Rules

[boxing] – *the set of rules commonly accepted in modern boxing*

Before this set of rules was put together by Arthur Graham Chambers and John Sholto Douglas in 1865 and introduced in 1867, boxing was on the whole a disorganised and brutal affair still fought with bare knuckles. The twelve different rules stipulated the use of a standard-sized 24-square-feet *ring*, three-minute rounds, a ten-second count, and the use of gloves for the first time. The rules take their name from Douglas, the 9th Marquess of *Queensberry*, who publicly endorsed them.

rabbit

[cricket] – *a poor batsman*

A *rabbit* is a batsman powerless to do anything when faced with the advancing bowler, similar to a rabbit caught in the headlights of an oncoming car. The term is sometimes also used to describe a particular batsman who is often dismissed by the same bowler. For example, Mike Atherton lost his wicket to Glenn McGrath nineteen times in his career – the most times any batsman has been dismissed by one bowler in international cricket history – earning him the label *Glenn McGrath's bunny*.

A *ferret* or *weasel* is an even worse batsman, based on them being sent in after a rabbit.

rabbit punch

[boxing] – *a punch to the back of the neck*

This is considered very dangerous because of the possible damage to the neck and spinal cord. As a result, it isn't allowed in boxing. It takes its name from the method used by hunters and farmers across the world to kill rabbits with a quick, hard strike to the back of the neck.

Rae's Creek

[golf] – *a creek that runs in front of the 12th green at the Augusta National Golf Club*

The creek also runs at the back of the 11th green and has a tributary near the tee at the 13th hole. It plays a very important role on the course, as the unfortunate American four-time **Masters** runner-up Tom Weiskopf found out to his cost at the tournament in 1980. On the 12th hole, he found the creek a record six times, shooting a 13 in the process.

The creek is connected to the Savannah River and named after John *Rae*, a well-known local who lived in the area in the 18th century. His house – the furthest up the Savannah River from Fort Augusta – was a much-needed safe haven for local residents during Indian attacks.

Rawalpindi Express

[cricket] – *a nickname for Pakistani cricketer Shoaib Akhtar*

Born on 13 August 1975 in Rawalpindi, Punjab, Shoaib Akhtar is the fastest recorded bowler the world has seen. So far, he's the first and only bowler to officially break the 100 mph barrier – achieving the milestone of 100.04 mph for the first time in a one-day international against New Zealand in 2002. Playing against England in the 2003 cricket World Cup, at 100.2 mph, he bowled the fastest official delivery ever unleashed by man.

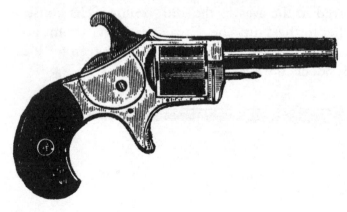

real tennis

[real tennis] – *a game played
with a racquet and ball in a court
reminiscent of medieval cloisters, with
either two or four players*

Initially known as *jeu de paume* (palm game),
the game is thought to have been invented
by French monks in monastery courtyards
in the 11th or 12th century, and is widely
considered as the predecessor of all modern
racquet and ball games. In time, it became
tennis – an adaptation of the word 'Tenez!'
('Take this!'), which the monks would shout
at each other before serving the ball. The
game quickly gained in popularity, and by
the 15th century, the nobility in England
and Scotland were modifying the courtyards
of their houses into suitable playing areas.

It became known as *real tennis* only at the end of
the 19th century, as a way of distinguishing it from
the recently invented, but increasingly popular, *lawn
tennis*.

red card

[football] – *the red-coloured card shown by a referee to a player to indicate that he is being dismissed from the pitch*

The concept of red and yellow cards for helping to officiate football matches was invented by English former referee and then chairman of the FIFA international referee committee, Kenneth George Aston. He was going about his business in the FIFA offices one day when a call came in from the 1966 World Cup tournament manager, querying whether Bobby and Jack Charlton had been cautioned in the England–Argentina match the previous day, in which the referee spoke only German. It turned out he'd just received a call from the Charlton brothers asking him to check – as the

first they knew of
their booking was
from reading the
Sunday papers over
breakfast.

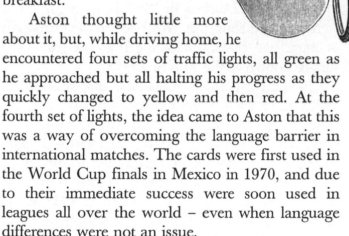

Aston thought little more
about it, but, while driving home, he
encountered four sets of traffic lights, all green as
he approached but all halting his progress as they
quickly changed to yellow and then red. At the
fourth set of lights, the idea came to Aston that this
was a way of overcoming the language barrier in
international matches. The cards were first used in
the World Cup finals in Mexico in 1970, and due
to their immediate success were soon used in
leagues all over the world – even when language
differences were not an issue.

Red Devils

[football] – *the nickname for Manchester United FC*

The club was founded in 1878 by workers of the Lancashire and Yorkshire Railway Company. They named it *Newton Heath LYR* and the club was soon nicknamed the *Heathens*. In 1902, however, the club were declared bankrupt, which led to the formation of *Manchester United*. Following this, the team was simply known as the *Reds* or *United*.

In the early 1950s, United manager Sir Matt Busby assembled a young, exciting and brilliant team, which the media quickly labelled the *Busby Babes*. Two league titles followed in 1956 and 1957. I have a very affectionate connection to this team, as England World Cup winner Nobby Stiles and myself were both signed by United in 1957 at the height of the Busby Babes' heyday (Nobby went on to sign professional forms and had a great career at Old Trafford, while my dad made me 'get a proper job first' before being happy that I play football for a living).

The quality and success of the team meant Busby had entered the club into the European Champions Cup each year from 1956. Tragically, in 1958, when the team were returning from a game abroad against Red Star Belgrade, their plane crashed while trying to take off at Munich airport. Seven players were killed and Busby was severely injured. Another member of the team, the great Duncan Edwards, died a fortnight later and a further two were sufficiently injured to never play again. Although Busby recovered to rebuild and manage the team again, the Busby Babes moniker was now wholly inappropriate and was dropped.

At the beginning of the 1960s, Salford Rugby Club toured France and because of their red shirts, became known as the *Red Devils*. Busby liked it, as he thought that opposing teams would find the name intimidating, and he adopted it for his own side. Devil logos soon made their way into match programmes and onto club scarves, and in 1970, the official club badge was redesigned to incorporate a devil holding a pitch-fork. Manchester United have been the Red Devils ever since.

ring

[boxing] – *the square area in which a bout takes place*

In the sport's early days, before the introduction of *rings* as we know them today, a group of spectators would form a circle around a fight as it unfolded. Those standing at the front would hold a rope as a way of marking out a ring. As boxing was illegal in many places at this point, it also allowed the fight organiser to get away if the police appeared, with only the loss of a bit of rope.

By the time more organised bouts and square fighting areas were introduced in the 19th century, the word 'ring' was fully engrained in boxing terminology and continued to be used.

Road Hole

[golf] – *the 461-yard, par-4 17th hole on the Old Course, St Andrews*

This is considered by many to be the hardest *par* 4 in the world. It starts with a blind drive over where the old tram shed once stood, now an outbuilding of the Old Course Hotel. Players usually pick out a letter from the hotel logo on the building wall as their line, but must choose wisely as the fairway narrows to under ten paces. A little too left and you will be in knee-high fescue, a little too right and you are out of bounds in the hotel's pond. Up ahead, however, the hole's greatest dangers lie in wait. First, there's the notorious *Road* bunker, which sits beside the green. It has destroyed many golfers' rounds over the years, notably Tommy Nakajima's at the 1978 Open – he took four to get out, leading to a quintuple-*bogey* nine.

If you clear what many locals still refer to as the *Sands of Nakajima* but fail to stop the ball on the green, you will find yourself on or over the old gravel turnpike road from which the hole takes its name. Land on it and you have to play off it, so kiss goodbye to the sole of your wedge. Land over it and the chances are your ball will be tucked up against the stone wall behind it, affording you no backswing.

Despite its innocuous name, the *Road Hole* is anything but easy.

rope-a-dope

[boxing] – *a tactic whereby a fighter feigns being trapped on the ropes, encouraging his opponent to hit him and consequently tire himself out*

Muhammad Ali used this tactic to great effect on several occasions during his career, notably making a *dope* of the undefeated Heavyweight Champion, George Foreman in Zaire, in the 1974 fight billed the *Rumble in the Jungle*. Ali let Foreman, possibly the hardest-hitting heavyweight in boxing history, unleash on him for several rounds. Then, according to Foreman, Ali whispered 'Is that all you got, George?' before knocking him out in the eighth round.

Ali named this strategy as *rope-a-dope* while being interviewed in the mid-1970s, long after he had employed it for the first time.

scorpion kick

[football] – *a peculiar move where a player jumps forward, places their hands on the ground and then kicks the ball away with their heels*

This term was given to an outrageous skill invented and perfected by Colombian goalkeeper René Higuita. Instead of catching a high incoming ball, he would allow it to go over his head, bringing both legs and feet upwards to make contact with the ball behind his back, producing a scorpion-like movement. The degree of difficulty is such that the technique is not just dangerous for any keeper, it's misguided. However it is, naturally, highly entertaining and when Higuita did do it, he rarely got it wrong. I actually noticed him practising the move during the pre-match warm-up before the England vs. Colombia international at Wembley in 1995, when he famously used it on a goal-bound ball from Jamie Redknapp to the delight and admiration of the predominantly English crowd. 'I call it my scorpion kick and I try to do it whenever possible', he explained afterwards.

show the bowler the maker's name

[cricket] – *to bat defensively with a straight bat*

Coaches traditionally shout this at batsmen while they practise in the nets. The best way to *show the bowler the maker's name* is to get on the front foot and point the face of the bat, where the manufacturer's logo usually is, straight back down the pitch at the bowler so he can read it. Doing this encourages the use of a straight bat, producing the most effective defensive shot available in the game.

What remains to be seen, however, is if this expression will survive the current transition in the modern game – whereby bats are used to advertise

anything and everything, and the maker's name is often removed in order to make space for a more lucrative sponsor. Before the International Cricket Council relaxed the rules on this, only the bat manufacturer or the batsmen themselves were meant to display logos on the bat. This led to the practice of large companies buying little bat factories and then producing a handful of bats a year, which meant they could send out batsmen to the middle wielding portable billboards.

silly point

[cricket] – *a fielding position very close to the batsman, square on the off-side*

As the name suggests, this is not a great place to be put by your captain. In the early days of cricket this position was known as *point of the bat* or *bat's end*. Over time, as it dawned on cricketers that standing so close to the bat as it was being swung was a peculiar thing to do, it became *silly point*; the fielder has to be silly to agree to stand there.

slam-dunk smash

[tennis] – *a smash hit high and early by a jumping player in mid-air*

This takes its name from both the standard over-head *smash*, a move that has been used in tennis since it began, and the basketball term *slam dunk*, whereby a player jumps in the air and powerfully and dramatically *dunks* the ball through the basket from close range to score, grabbing onto the hoop with both hands. In tennis, *slam-dunk smash* was coined for the move frequently employed and made famous in the 1990s by the record fourteen-time **Grand Slam** winner, Pete Sampras.

sledging

[cricket] – *barracking of the batsmen by the fielding side in order to disturb their concentration*

The Australians are known to be some of the most prolific and effective *sledgers* in the game, and so it's fitting that the term originates from their country. It's thought that in the 1960s, a fast bowler from New South Wales called Graham Corling made an awful faux pas at a party in front of mixed company. Someone promptly told him that he was 'as subtle as a sledgehammer'. Apparently, this was then abbreviated to *sledgehammer*, and then *sledge*. A further connection was made to the song 'When a Man Loves a Woman', by Percy Sledge, and Corling acquired the nickname *Percy*.

Although the practice of verbally abusing batsmen has been around since cricket began, it was becoming more widespread at the beginning of the 1970s, and so those familiar with the story called it sledging.

In spite of their sledging prowess, the Australians have also been the victims of some great retorts over the years. Take Jimmy Ormond's Ashes exchange with Mark Waugh. The Australian asked Ormond what a man of his lowly cricketing stature was doing out in the middle. 'I may not be the best cricketer in the world', responded Ormond, 'but at least I'm the best cricketer in my family'.

Or there was Zimbabwean Eddo Brandes' discussion with Glenn McGrath, after Brandes had played and missed at another McGrath delivery. 'Oi, Brandes, why are you so f**ing fat?' enquired McGrath. 'Because every time I f**k your wife, she gives me a biscuit', he replied. Even the Australians were in hysterics.

snooker

[snooker] – *a game played with fifteen red and six other coloured balls and a cue on a baize-covered table with pockets*

Although billiards dates back to the beginning of the 15th century, this game was invented much later in 1875 – when some British Army officers of a Devonshire regiment and their Colonel, Sir Neville Chamberlain (no relation of the later Prime Minister) were bored at their Mess while posted in Jubbulpore, India. Soon after, a young subaltern arrived at the regiment, bringing the term *snooker* – used for new recruits at the Royal Military Academy where he had trained. Later, while playing the as-yet-unnamed game, an officer missed an easy pot, prompting Chamberlain to call him a snooker. Both the game and its new name were spread across the British Empire by the movement of the military that played it.

soccer

[football] – *a name for football that is predominantly used in the US, among other countries*

The Football Association was formed in London in 1863 from a meeting of eleven clubs and schools to establish the laws of the game. One of the rules distinctly prohibited the carrying of the ball, and the sport required a name to distinguish it from rugby football, so *Association Football* was chosen. But on the whole, people found this long-winded and abbreviated it to *socca*. It was then adapted to *socker*, before *soccer* was finally settled on by the end of the 19th century. It's thought to have evolved with public school and University students, most notably from Oxford, thanks to their propensity to shorten words and then add *-er*. Rugby was also afforded a similar treatment at the time, becoming *rugger*.

I'm glad to say it's rarely used in this country any more, as I prefer the more self-explanatory *football*. Soccer was, however, also adopted by the US, and they still use the name as a way of differentiating the sport from both rugby and, more importantly for them, the sport of American football.

southpaw

[boxing] – *a left-hander, and therefore a boxer who leads with his right hand*

In America, as the game of baseball evolved, people realised that ballparks should be designed so that the more common right-handed batter would face east in order to avoid the late afternoon or early evening sun shining in his eyes. This meant that the pitcher would face west, but if he was left-handed, he would be throwing with his south-side hand, or *southpaw*. In time, the term came to represent left-handers in sport in general, and it was adopted by American boxing before making its way across the Atlantic to Britain in the mid-19th century.

The Australian equivalent is a *mollydooker*.

squash

[squash] – *a racquet-and-ball sport played by two or four people on a court surrounded by four walls*

Although there had been many racquet-and-ball games in existence in Britain since the Middle Ages, *squash* was not invented until much more recently. At the beginning of the 19th century, bored inmates of Fleet Prison on London's South Bank invented the game of *racquets* while spending their days hitting balls against the walls of their cells with makeshift racquets. Strangely enough, the game was then picked up by Harrow School on the other side of London, around 1820. About ten years later, some pupils were playing racquets when the ball they were playing with punctured. In spite of this, they continued to play, discovering that as the ball *squashed* on impact with the wall, it created a very different game. Their invention proved popular among pupils and staff alike, and the first four squash courts were built at the school in 1864.

Stableford

[golf] – *a type of competition in which the scoring system is based on a player's handicap and the stroke index of each hole*

You get one point for a net **bogey**, two points for a net **par**, three points for a net **birdie**, four points for a net **eagle** and five for a net **albatross**. Add all your points up at the end and the player with the most wins. Simple! And so thought Dr Frank Barney Gorton *Stableford* when he invented the system at Wallasey Golf Club in 1931.

Before serving as a major in the Great War, Stableford had had a handicap of plus one, but by the time he returned his handicap had slipped to 8. This, coupled with Wallasey's notoriously strong winds, meant he found it almost impossible to reach the greens of the long par-4s in two, which infuriated him enormously, until he devised the system still used by many club golfers today: 'I was practising on the second fairway at Wallasey Golf Club one day in the latter part of 1931 when the thought ran through my mind that many players in competitions got very little fun since they tore up their cards after playing only a few holes, and I wondered if anything could be done about it.' Wallasey held the first Stableford competition on 16 May 1932.

steeplechase

[horse racing] – *a race of between two and four-and-a-half miles in length, over fences that are a minimum of four-and-a-half feet high*

In Ireland in 1752, 'a certain Mr Callaghan and his friend, Mr Edmund Blake, made a sporting wager to race cross country from Buttevant Church to the steeple of Saint Leger Church, a distance of roughly four-and-a-half miles'. This extract from a document found in the library of Dromoland Castle is believed to be an account of the birth of the *steeplechase* – a race in which orientation of the course was originally by churches and their steeples. This usually entailed negotiating whatever obstacles the countryside had to offer and, although this notion of diverse fences and ditches remains, the orientation by church does not. In spite of this, races such as the Grand National are still known as *steeplechases*.

sticky dog

[cricket] – *a wet pitch*

When a pitch has been rained on, it becomes soft and *sticky*, making it a *dog* to bat on. *Sticky dogs* are no longer a feature of top-flight cricket, as pitches are covered immediately when it begins to rain – but in the past, they were very much a part of the game. A drying wicket would lend itself perfectly to certain bowlers, notably England's Derek Underwood, who gained the nickname of *Deadly* for the havoc he could wreak in such situations. The Ashes series of 1968 saw England go to the last Test at the **Oval** one-nil down. Nevertheless, they dictated the final match and looked set for victory on the last session of the series when a violent thunderstorm seemed to bring Australian salvation. The game finally resumed, giving England one last gasp at squaring the series. Underwood proceeded to take four wickets in 27 balls – securing victory with five minutes to spare and bringing about one of the most dramatic conclusions to a Test in cricketing history.

stumps

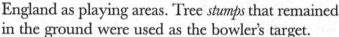

*[cricket] – the three wooden sticks
which the batsman must protect from
the bowling*

When cricket was first played in the
13th century, its early practitioners
used the cleared forests of Southern
England as playing areas. Tree *stumps* that remained
in the ground were used as the bowler's target.

Stumps have progressed somewhat since
then, seeing the introduction of built-in cameras
in the early 1990s and, more recently, stump
microphones. Some players see these microphones
as a regression, however, as they hinder their
ability to **sledge** opposing batsmen while out in the
middle. That didn't stop Australian wicketkeeper
Ian Healy from the act – when stockily-built Sri
Lankan Arjuna Ranatunga asked for a runner
during a one-day international, Healy was picked
up on the mic suggesting that 'You don't get a
runner for being an overweight, unfit, fat, f**k.'

stymie

[golf] – *a situation in which the path to the flag is blocked*

This term is now applied to any shot when there is something obstructing your intended route to the target, but it comes more specifically from a rule that was abolished in 1951. Nowadays, if an opponent's ball blocks your path on the green you can ask them to mark it. But before then, if their ball blocked your path you were *stymied*; it was tough luck – you had to play into it, over it or around it. The one exception was if the two balls were less than six inches apart, in which case the non-striker would lift their ball and replace it once the striker had putted. This is why many scorecards at that time measured six inches across.

Stymies used to play a significant role in the outcome of many matches, notably the final round of the Amateur Championship at St Andrews in 1930. On the first extra hole in a play-off with Cyril Tolley, the great Bobby Jones left his **birdie** putt a couple of inches from the cup in the line of his opponent's ball. It was the perfect *stymie* and secured him victory. Later that year, he went on to win the Open Championship, the US Open, and the US Amateur Championship, completing the original **Grand Slam** – this phenomenal achievement all started with a stymie!

The word itself derives from the Old Scottish vernacular for a person with little spiritual belief, or someone who has difficulty 'seeing the light', similarly to a stymied golfer who has difficulty seeing the hole.

sweeper

[football] – *a player who roams behind the defenders without specific man-marking duties*

The idea of this position is that the player will *sweep up* any problems that should arise if the line of orthodox defenders is breached. Because of the fluidity of the *sweeper*'s role in comparison with other defenders, the position is also referred to as the *libero*, the Italian word for *free*. Finding a player clever enough to maximise this role is the key. I always admired the great two-time European Footballer of the Year Franz Beckenbauer's ability to clear up at the back, but also to break forward and truly maximise the free role. His command of the ball and play was unrivalled in that position at the time, and so saw him affectionately nicknamed *Emperor Franz* and *The Kaiser*.

sweet science

[boxing] – *the art or practice of boxing*

Over a century before the introduction of the **Queensberry Rules** and the consequent coordination of boxing as a whole, the British champion of the time, Jack Broughton, had formulated the sport's first code in the form of the *London Prize Ring Rules*. Motivated by the untimely death of one of his opponents during a bout in 1743, he created the regulations in the hope of turning boxing into a more definite science. A little later, in 1818, English writer Pierce Egan referred to the sport as 'the *sweet science* of bruising' in *Boxiana; or Sketches of Modern Pugilism*, his collection of boxing articles. The term was finally adopted and popularised by sportswriters around the mid-20th century, notably by the much admired American journalist A.J. Liebling – who named his own first collection of boxing articles *The Sweet Science* in Egan's honour.

Toffeemen

[football] – *the nickname for Everton FC*

The *Toffeemen* or *Toffees* have been the established nicknames for the club from its very early days and are likely to have come about as a result of the following story. Many early club meetings were held at the Queen's Head Hotel, which was near Ye Anciente Everton Toffee House run by a woman known as Old Ma Bushell. She produced *Everton Toffees*, which she sold in large numbers to the fans that came to watch Everton play in the new Football League. However, in 1892, the club moved from Anfield to Goodison Park, displacing her market and consequently reducing her sales to nothing.

Instead, near the new ground was Mother Noblett's Toffee Shop, but Mother Noblett couldn't take advantage of her new-found bit of fortune, as Old Ma Bushell had patented the Everton Toffee. So Mother Noblett created the Everton Mint, which – with the black and white stripes of an earlier Everton strip – was a huge success.

Refusing to be beaten by the creative Mrs Noblett, Old Ma Bushell successfully persuaded the club to let her distribute her Everton Toffees to the fans inside the ground before kick-off. She employed the services of her beautiful grand-daughter Jemima Bushell who, wearing her best hat and dress, went around the ground with a basket full of toffees. So the tradition of the Everton Toffee Lady – which remains to this day – was born.

total football

[football] – *a system whereby if a player moves out of position, their role is filled by a team-mate, leaving the formation intact*

The term was coined principally to describe the style of play of the great Dutch national side of the 1970s. The strategy required a *total* level of fitness and a gamut of skills from each and every outfield player, as they all had to be able to move to, and play in, each other's positions at any given moment.

I came face to face with *total football* at both club and country level. Playing for Arsenal, I faced the great Ajax who also perfected the system, winning and losing against the Dutch side in European competition. As Scotland goalkeeper, in my second full international appearance and playing against Holland, I was on the losing side, beaten 2-1 in the last minute by the team who went on to become World Cup runners-up in 1974. While Johann Cruyff was the star at executing the system, its mastermind was the brilliant coach/manager, the late Rinus Michels. Otherwise known as *The General* for both his hardline approach as a coach and his famous comment that 'football is war', Michels' success and impact on the game saw him named Coach of the Century by FIFA in 1999.

Valley of Sin

[golf] – *a deep hollow just in front of the 18th green on the Old Course at St Andrews*

This 357-yard, par-4 last hole isn't a difficult one, as long as you avoid the *Valley of Sin*. Depending on where the pin has been cut, the drive should usually be aimed at the clock on the Royal and Ancient Clubhouse, setting you up with an approach shot over the Valley. Many people attempt to drive the green in one, and it's this that gives the hollow its name: the notion that they have succumbed to temptation and now find themselves in the Valley of Sin.

Four-time Open champion Tom Morris Snr. designed the green and its adjoining hollow in 1865, and regarded it as his finest work. Apparently, he would often stand and watch with pride players on the green, from the window of his shop just across the street.

Vardon grip

[golf] – *an overlapping grip on the golf club*

This way of holding the club takes its name from the great English champion Harry Vardon (1870–1937). He didn't invent the grip, but as golf's first international celebrity, he certainly popularised it. He was also the first professional golfer to play in knickerbockers, dress shirt, tie and buttoned jacket, and despite his cumbersome attire, he won the Open six times – a record that remains to this day. The credibility that he gave the grip ensured that it's one still used by the vast majority of golfers in today's game. Perhaps we should all reconsider, though, as stars such as Jack Nicklaus and Tiger Woods use the interlocking grip instead.

Wallabies

[rugby union] – *the nickname for the Australian national team*

In 1905, the New Zealand rugby team had made their first tour of Britain and acquired the name **All Blacks** from the British press. In 1908, the Australian rugby team embarked on their first tour of Britain and again, the press felt that the visitors needed a name. Initially, they became the *Rabbits* – but the Australians disliked being called what was to them an imported pest. Instead, they chose and pushed for the native *Wallabies*, which the British press subsequently used.

Originally, only members of touring teams were called Wallabies, but since the 1980s, the name has been used for all players who represent Australia, regardless of whether they play at home or abroad.

Whispering Death

[cricket] – *the nickname for West Indian fast bowler, Michael Holding*

He was one of the fastest bowlers of his generation, devastating batting line-ups across the world throughout the 1970s and early 80s. His name is perfectly explained by *Wisden's* Mike Selvey: '[His run] began intimidatingly far away. He turned, and began the most elegant long-striding run of them all, feet kissing the turf silently, his head turning gently and ever so slightly from side to side, rhythmically, like that of a cobra hypnotising its prey. Good batsmen tended not to watch him all the way lest they became mesmerised. To the umpires he was malevolent stealth personified so they christened him *Whispering Death.*'

yellow jersey

[cycling] – *the jersey worn by the overall leader of the Tour de France*

The Tour de France was founded as a marketing stunt for a French newspaper called *L'Auto*, by its editor and co-founder, Henri Desgrange, back in 1902. Held annually, the race, and consequently the circulation of *L'Auto*, went from strength to strength. During the 1919 Tour, on the rest day in Luchon, it occurred to Desgrange that the race leader should wear something distinctive to ensure all spectators knew who was winning. On 10 July 1919, he announced that it was to be a *yellow jersey*, a decision he had reached because of the yellow paper *L'Auto* was printed on. Mercantile as it was, he had created one of the most famous icons in sport.

yips

[golf] – *a psychological syndrome that affects a golfer's technique, especially when putting*

This mental affliction can profoundly affect a golfer's career. A head-on collision with a Greyhound bus nearly brought the great Ben Hogan's career to an end, but it didn't. The *yips* did. The term was conceived over 70 years ago by another sufferer – the Open, US Open and USPGA winner Tommy Armour. He used 'yips' to describe 'that ghastly time when with the first movement of the putter, the golfer blacks out, loses sight of the ball and hasn't the remotest idea of what to do with the putter or, occasionally, that he is holding a putter at all'.

There are similar afflictions in other sports, notably darts, in which players can totally lose control of the dart they are throwing, and in more severe cases can't let go of the dart at all. This is known as *dartitis* and its most famous sufferer was five-times World Champion, Eric Bristow.

yorker

[cricket] – *a delivery that pitches on the popping crease*

This is a very difficult ball for a batsman to play. It's most usually and successfully deployed sparingly as a surprise weapon, often being executed as a slower ball. The aim of the *yorker* is to deceive the batsman in the flight. As a result, it takes its name from the 18th-century colloquialism to *york* or to *pull yorkshire* on someone, meaning to trick or mislead.

Australians call it a *sandshoe crusher* or a *toe crusher*.

zooter

[cricket] – *a delivery by a leg-spinner, slipped out of the hand with little or no spin on it, but which dips in to the batsman late in flight*

The name for this delivery was introduced by Shane Warne and his bowling coach and mentor, Terry Jenner. Some think they gave it a name so it could be added to the list of other named deliveries in his arsenal such as the *flipper* and *slider*, just to enhance his aura of mystery, and consequently to create more doubt in a batsman's mind as to what they will face when he bowls.

There is no doubt that Warne is one of the greatest bowlers the world has ever seen, but spin in the non-cricketing sense (according to the motto that all publicity is good publicity) has also always been a strength of his, and this is part of his appeal. A drugs ban, the **Ball of the Century**, a record number of Test wickets, and tabloid scandals on the front and back pages have all added to the media frenzy surrounding Warne – assigning him sufficient celebrity to earn the nickname *Hollywood*.

Index

athletics
Fosbury flop 74
marathon 116

badminton 12

boules
carreau 42

boxing
Brockton Blockbuster 29
haymaker 95
Louisville Lip 108
Palooka 138
Queensberry Rules 148
rabbit punch 150
ring 158
rope-a-dope 160
southpaw 170
sweet science 179

canoeing
Eskimo roll 71

cricket 52
bails 14
Ball of the Century 15

beamer 18
bodyline 25
bumper 32
Bunsen 33
chin music 44
Chinaman 45
corridor of uncertainty
    49
cow corner 50
devil's number 60
Doctor 61
doosra 63
dot ball 65
duck 66
Duckworth-Lewis
    method 67
flipper 72
googly 82
gully 88
hat-trick 94
Little Master 104
Lord's 107
maiden 113
mankad 114
Michelle 119
Nelson 123
nightwatchman 124

Oval 136
pair of spectacles 137
Pigeon 140
popping crease 144
pyjama cricket 147
rabbit 149
Rawalpindi Express 152
show the bowler the
    maker's name 162
silly point 164
sledging 166
sticky dog 174
stumps 175
Whispering Death 186
yorker 189
zooter 190

croquet 55

curling 57
bonspiel 27

cycling
autobus 11
broom wagon 31
domestique 62
King of the Mountains
    99
lanterne rouge 100
Madison 112

on the rivet 133
yellow jersey 187

darts
Annie's room 10
bed and breakfast 19
madhouse 111
Milky Bar Kid 120
Nine Dart 126
oche 129

football
Addicks 4
Bhoys 20
Black Cats 23
cap 40
Cruyff turn 56
golden goal 79
Gunners 89
hand of God 92
local derby 105
nutmeg 128
Old Firm 131
red card 154
Red Devils 156
scorpion kick 161
soccer 169
sweeper 178
Toffeemen 180
total football 182

golf 80
albatross 5
Amen Corner 8
Big Easy 21
birdie 22
bogey 26
brassie 28
Burma Road 35
caddie 36
Calamity Jane 37
Claret Jug 46
dormie 64
eagle 68
Eisenhower Tree 70
fore 73
Golden Bear 78
Grand Slam 85
Green Jacket 87
Hell Bunker 96
links 102
mashie niblick 117
Masters 118
mulligan 121
nineteenth hole 127
out of the screws 135
par 139
Postage Stamp 145
Rae's Creek 151
Road Hole 159
Stableford 172

stymie 176
Valley of Sin 183
Vardon grip 184
yips 188

gymnastics
Gaylord flip 77

hockey 97

horse racing
Burlington Bertie 34
carpet 41
Derby 58
furlong 75
jockey 98
steeplechase 173

lacrosse 101

miscellaneous
Croke Park 54

motor racing
cockpit 48
Eau Rouge 69
Grand Prix 84
pits 141
pole position 142

octopush 130

pool 143

real tennis 153

rowing
catch a crab 43
coxswain 51

rugby union
All Blacks 6
Barbarians 17
Calcutta Cup 38
Garryowen 76
haka 91
Lions 103
on the hoof 132
Pumas 146
Wallabies 185

ski-jumping
outjump the hill 134

snooker 168
cocked hat 47

squash 171

tennis
bagel job 13
deuce 59
Grand Slam 85
love 110
slam-dunk smash 165

wrestling
Greco-Roman 83

The Hamster
Revolution

How to Manage Your Email
Before it Manages You

The Hamster Revolution

Mike Song
Vicki Halsey
Tim Burress

BERRETT-KOEHLER PUBLISHERS, INC.
San Francisco
www.bk-life.com

Patent Pending COTA System - CKS

Berrett-Koehler Publishers, Inc.

235 Montgomery Street. Suite 650

San Francisco, CA 94104-2916

Tel: 415-288-0260 Fax: 415-362-2512 www.bkconnection.com

Ordering Information

Quantity sales. Special discounts are available on quantity purchases by corporations, associations, and others. For details, contact the "Special Sales Department" at the Berrett-Koehler address above.

Individual sales. Berrett-Koehler publications are available through most bookstores. They can also be ordered direct from Berrett-Koehler: Tel: (800) 929-2929; Fax (802) 864-7626.

Orders for college textbook/course adoption use. Please contact Berrett-Koehler: Tel: (800) 929-2929; Fax (802) 864-7626.

Orders by U.S. trade bookstores and wholesalers. Please contact Publishers Group West, 1700 Fourth Street, Berkeley, CA 94710. Tel: (510) 528-1444; Fax (510) 528-3444

Berrett-Koehler and BK logo are registered trademarks of Berrett-Koehler Publishers, Inc.

Printed in the United States of America

Berrrret-Koehler books are printed on long-lasting acid-free paper. When it is available, we choose paper that has been manufactured by environmentally responsible processes. These may include using trees grown in sustainable forests, incorporating recycled paper, minimizing chlorine in bleaching, or recycling the energy produced at the paper mill.

Library of Congress Cataloging-in-Publication Data

Song, Mike, 1964-

The hamster revolution: how to manage email before it manages you / by Mike Song, Vicki Halsey, and Tim Burress.

    p. cm.

Includes bibliographical references.

ISBN-13: 978-1-57675-437-5 (hardcover)

1. Electronic mail messages –Management. 2. Personal information management. I. Halsey, Vicki, 1955-II. Burress, Tim, 1964-III. Title.

TK5105.73.S66 2007

651.7'9 —dc22

                         2006024284

First Edition

12 11 10 09 08 07   10 9 8 7 6 5 4 3

Producer: Tolman Creek Design LLC, Copy Editor: Patricia Brewer, Proof Reader: Ginny Munroe, Indexer: Shan Young

The productivity of knowledge work — still abysmally low — will become the economic challenge of the knowledge society. On it will depend the competitive position of every single country, every single industry, and every single institution within society.

—Peter Drucker

....

Every generation needs a new revolution.

—Thomas Jefferson

For Kristin Song, Richard Halsey, and Daphne Burress

Thanks for believing.

Contents

Foreword   xi

1   Confessions of an Info-Hamster   1

2   A New Way to Work   5

3   Email Adds Up!   11

4   Strategy 1: Reduce Email Volume   17

5   A Tale of Two Emails   35

6   Strategy 2: Improve Email Quality   41

7   Strategy 3: Info-Coaching Sustains Results   53

8   Help! It's Not So Easy!   65

9   Harold's Progress Check   69

10   Chaos in Info-Land   73

11   Strategy 4: File and Find It Fast With COTA   81

12   A Blue Sky Wrap Up   97

Epilogue   105

Appendix 1: Fast Answers for Busy Hamsters   107

Appendix 2: Case Study: Capital One's Email
Efficiency Solution   113

Notes   119

Acknowledgements   120

Index   122

Services Available   126

About the Authors   128

Foreword

Every once in awhile, the business world teeters off balance. This usually happens when events converge to create an absurd situation or *incongruity*. Invariably, an *incongruity* is a big opportunity. In the 1980s, the incongruity was that managers lacked a simple system for managing people. When the rubber met the road, most lacked the people skills needed to maximize performance. Along came *The One Minute Manager®* and suddenly millions of professionals had a book that *simplified the management of people*. Twenty years later, I'm thrilled that it continues to help managers manage and leaders lead.

In the 1990s, the *incongruity* was that people lacked a simple strategy for managing change. This was absurd because the '90s were a time of great upheaval in the business world. Along came Spencer Johnson's *Who Moved My Cheese?®* and suddenly millions of professionals had a book that *simplified the management of change*.

Today, the *incongruity* is that you're asked to process more information, particularly email, than is humanly possible. Each day you multitask your way through an avalanche of disorganized, unstructured information. It's a stressful world filled with uncertainty and interruptions. That said, I have some very good news. Just when you need it most, along comes *The Hamster Revolution* with four highly effective strategies for *simplifying the management of information*.

You'll love this book for three reasons:

1. **It Works:** *The Hamster Revolution* contains practical and proven insights that will make you more effective the next time you sit down at your computer.

2. **It's a Valuable Guide for Leaders:** Email now consumes a quarter of the day for the typical professional. If you aspire to be a great leader or team player, you have to develop a strategy for managing email. *The Hamster Revolution* provides clear guidance on how to do just that.

3. **It's Fast and Fun:** Let me guess—you're busy, right? Sometimes you barely have time to think, let alone read a long book filled with thousands of tips. Relax. You can read this book in about 90 minutes. The authors focus on "a *small number* of *high-impact* email insights." You're going to smile when you meet the book's star: Harold. He's a funny guy and in some ways, he'll remind you… of you.

I'd like to congratulate you for being here, right now in this moment. You've envisioned something that many of your colleagues and competitors have yet to discover: *You can't unlock your fullest potential when you and your team are drowning in email.* It's time to address the *incongruity* of email overload. It's time for the next big revolution to begin. So cue the lights and quiet on the set. Here comes Harold and *The Hamster Revolution*!

Ken Blanchard
Co-author, *The One Minute Manager*®

1

CONFESSIONS OF AN INFO-HAMSTER

I was working peacefully in my office when the door slowly opened and shut with a click. I looked up but no one was there. "You'd better be able to help me!" said a small voice. *Was this a joke?*

I stood up and *that's* when I saw him. Trudging across the floor, tugging on his tie, was a small, nervous-looking white hamster with brown spots. He was wearing a dark blue business suit and carrying a small black briefcase. He looked tired and defeated.

"I hear you're the so-called productivity expert," he said. "I'm Harold."

I leaned down to shake his paw, "Pleased to meet you, Harold. And yes, my passion is helping professionals lead more productive and fulfilling lives."

Harold raised his eyes hopefully. "Maybe I'm in the right place after all," he muttered.

Once I'd gotten over my initial shock that Harold was a hamster, I realized that he was my 1:30 PM appointment.

"Welcome, Harold! Please sit down and tell me what brings you here."

Harold hopped into a chair facing my desk. As he leaned back, his wireless personal digital assistant (PDA) buzzed loudly. Harold looked down at it, lost his balance, and almost fell through the gap in the back of the chair. He scrambled frantically to keep from falling and eventually regained his composure.

"Okay, okay. Here's my story. Five years ago, I landed my dream job: Human Resources Director at Foster and Schrubb Financial. At first, the position was perfect. I was incredibly productive and my team launched several big initiatives." Harold frowned and shifted in his seat, "But a couple of years ago, I noticed that I was working harder and harder and getting less and less done."

"How'd that feel?"

"Am I in analysis or something?" quipped Harold, rolling his eyes. "Well, Dr. Freud, I felt stressed. I was getting buried alive by email, voice mail, and meeting notes. I had information coming out of my ears."

Harold pointed at the PDA clipped to his belt. "Then I got this thing. At first I liked being connected 24-7, but soon I fell even further behind and…"

"Yes?"

"To make matters worse," Harold said softly as he picked at some loose fur on his wrist, "and this is embarrassing to admit," he leaned forward and whispered, "Lately, I'm having trouble finding stuff."

I leaned forward and whispered, "What kind of *stuff*, Harold?"

"Well, I'll store an email and when I really need it — I can't find it! Things just vaporize! And don't get me started on my team's shared storage drive; everyone's storing documents differently; no one knows how to clean it up; it's a mess! I spend a lot of time requesting resends and recreating documents that are missing. I'm staying late just to keep up."

"So work is spilling over into your personal life?"

Harold raised his furry eyebrows thoughtfully. He reached into his pocket and produced an impossibly small picture. I squinted and saw that it was Harold's family: a lovely wife and two beautiful children.

"Nice family."

"Upset family," corrected Harold wearily. "Thanks to wireless technology, I'm always online. Carol's really frustrated with the amount of time I spend working after-hours."

He held up his paws with an exasperated look. "The kids hate it when I do email on Saturday or Sunday. But part of me actually looks forward to weekends just so I can catch up on work. Sometimes, I miss a soccer game or dance recital but if I don't keep up..." Harold shrugged his little hamster shoulders as if to say, "*I just don't know anymore.*"

"So your dream job's become a nightmare?"

Harold nodded. "I feel like I'm losing... me."

He continued quietly, "I used to love learning new things. I was thrilled to get to the office each morning. Now I dread it. I feel like... like..." Harold struggled for the right words.

"Like a hamster on a wheel?" I offered.

"Yes!" shouted Harold, bolting upright in his chair, "I've become a *hamster on a wheel!* Running faster and harder, but getting nowhere."

I suddenly realized that Harold was unaware that he'd actually turned into a hamster. Although I'd helped countless professionals who felt and acted like hamsters, Harold was the first that actually *changed* into one! Apparently his metamorphosis had been so gradual that he hadn't noticed.

Harold paused and let out a deep sigh. "When I was younger, I had a much different vision of how my life would unfold."

"Tell me about that."

Harold raised his eyebrows and stared at the ground. He looked like he was trying to recall a distant memory.

"Well, I dreamed I'd have this really fulfilling job. I pictured myself surrounded by brilliant people working on these high-level, high-impact team projects — exciting stuff, life-changing stuff. I also imagined that I'd have much more time with my family, to laugh with friends, work out, garden, reflect." Harold smiled wryly, "I never thought I'd spend every waking hour stressing over email and feeling like a hamster on a wheel."

2

A NEW WAY TO WORK

Harold raised his paws in frustration. "So you're the expert. How do I get off the wheel?"

"You fight back, Harold. There's a better way to work."

"Yeah, yeah," he said looking tense, "I've taken a couple time-management classes, but they didn't help."

"Harold, this isn't a *time*-management problem. It's an *information*-management problem."

"It is?"

"Yes! Too much email and information is gushing into your life. Don't get me wrong; email is an amazing communication tool. But suddenly, it's keeping a lot of people from getting things done. Most professionals feel like they're stuck on a nonstop wheel-of-information overwhelm."

"So what's the answer?" asked Harold, sounding frustrated.

"Join *The Hamster Revolution.*"

"Huh?" asked Harold looking surprised. "Revolution against what?"

"Info-glut!" I said. "That's your enemy: way too much low-value information mucking up your world. You can't reach your fullest potential when you're drowning in email! *The Hamster Revolution* is a strategic plan that helps you conquer info-glut once and for all. Interested in learning more?"

"Sure," said Harold, looking both interested and worried at the same time.

I handed Harold a single sheet of paper, "Here's our schedule."

The Hamster Revolution Plan

Week 1 (Today): Email Insights (90 Minutes)
  Strategy 1: Reduce email volume
  Strategy 2: Improve email quality
  Strategy 3: Coach others to send you more actionable email

Week 2: Information Storage Insights (60 Minutes)
  Strategy 4: File and find info fast with COTA©

Week 3: Wrap-Up Meeting (30 Minutes)

Harold studied the schedule and seemed pleased, "Three hours works for me. I don't have a lot of time for this."

I nodded. "Today, we'll focus on streamlining the flow of email through your life. This will help you become more relaxed and effective at work. Sound good?"

"Wonderful, if I could actually do it," replied Harold cautiously.

"Don't worry. Our goal today is to concentrate on a *small* number of *high-impact* email insights. By the way, you won't have to write anything down because each Hamster Revolution strategy will be summarized by an easy-to-use tool."

"Four strategies and four tools… that's good," stated Harold emphatically. "But what exactly is next week's meeting about? What is COTA?"

"A moment ago you mentioned that you were having trouble finding things?"

"Sure."

"What if you could file and find all of your email, documents, and links in a flash?"

"That would be a miracle," said Harold softly.

"I can't promise you a miracle, but I've seen amazing results from people who've adopted an organizational system called COTA. COTA is a simple yet effective way to arrange your files and folders. After the COTA session, we'll give you a week to put all four strategies into practice on the job. During that week, you can call me anytime for coaching or feedback. Okay?"

Harold thought for a moment, "Seems like a workable plan so far."

We'll hold a third and final wrap-up meeting to see how you did. We can fine-tune your newly found Hamster Revolution skills and answer any lingering questions."

Harold leaned forward, "So it's kind of like a one-two punch? First we get email under control, and then we use this COTA thing to organize my information?"

I nodded. "We've discovered that there's a powerful *connection* between email efficiency and the way you store your info."

"What kind of connection?"

"Here are just a few examples:

- Reduced email volume means less email to store.

- Clear email subject lines make it easier to relocate stored email.

- A highly effective folder system helps you rapidly file email and documents. This reduces inbox overload.

- Responding to an email requesting info is a lot easier when you can find your info fast.

- There's also a time connection. Together, email and information storage tasks consume over 40% of a typical professional's day. [1, 2] When both of these activities become more efficient, your overall productivity takes a giant leap forward."

Harold raised his eyebrows. "So I need to improve *both* email and information storage to get off the hamster wheel?"

I nodded. "We're going to get your life back, Harold."

"I'll believe it when I see it," said Harold. "But I like your approach. You're looking at the whole process of managing information, not just email by itself. I've never thought of it that way before."

"You're not alone. Most professionals lack an effective plan for managing all the information flooding into their lives. To make matters worse, over the past five years, the volume of information we process has skyrocketed. For example, email volume is rising at a rate of 14.6% per year." [3]

Harold groaned, "I'm doomed."

"As inboxes and computer filing systems have become bloated, millions of professionals have begun to feel like hamsters. *Well, it's time for the hamsters to fight back!* The Hamster Revolution will restore order and control to your life. Best of all, it will save you 15 days a year."

Harold looked surprised, "15 days?"

"You can save a lot of time by mastering the flow of information through your world. So what do you think?"

Harold reflected on his predicament for a moment. Suddenly, with a determined look, he blurted, "Okay, I'll join your Hamster Revolution!"

"*Our* revolution," I smiled, "Ready to reclaim your life?"

Harold stood up on his chair and gave a mock salute. "Let the revolting begin!"

3

EMAIL ADDS UP!

As Harold saluted, Emilio, our Senior VP of Finance, walked past my door. His mouth dropped as he spied a tiny, saluting hamster teetering on a chair. He was so distracted that he crashed into a bank of filing cabinets, making a loud noise. Hoping that Harold wouldn't notice, I launched into one of my favorite topics: The True Cost of Email Overload.

"I love coffee, Harold. To be specific, I love Blue Sky mochaccinos, an irresistible blend of coffee, cream, and rich chocolate."

"We have a Blue Sky Café in our building, too," said Harold, looking confused.

"Well, several years ago I noticed that I was buying two or three cups of coffee a day. We were trying to trim the family budget so that we could save for our kids' college education. Just for kicks, I decided to calculate what those mochaccinos were costing me. It was more than $3,000 a year! Over time, I was literally spending my kids' college tuition on coffee!"

Harold shot me a look that said, "*What does this have to do with email?*"

"Email is a lot like coffee, Harold. It's kind of addicting and it definitely adds up."

"Addicting?" asked Harold, looking puzzled.

"Has your email system crashed in the past year?"

Harold nodded. "I did have a problem last month and it felt terrible. I was petrified that I was missing something important and I felt totally cut off from the world. I was really cranky and — looking back — I completely overreacted."

"The symptoms you describe sound like what I experience when I don't get coffee for a couple days. Those are feelings of withdrawal, Harold. Email occasionally brings us exciting and important information. Perhaps those emotional highs trigger something in our minds that makes us want to check it all the time."

"Sometimes I wind up doing email even when I have much more important things to do," noted Harold.

"Exactly, another reason we default to email is that it's easy and nonconfrontational. It's easier to zip off a critical email than it is to conduct a difficult live conversation with a colleague who is underperforming. Don't get me wrong. Email is a great productivity tool, but we're overusing it and in some cases — we're abusing it."

"Never thought of it that way," agreed Harold.

"Do you know how much email costs you each year?"

"Well isn't that the beauty of email? It's free. No stamps! " smirked Harold.

"We'll see," I replied. "How much time do you spend on email each year?"

Harold shook his head, "I have no idea. I guess I get about 50 a day and I probably hit the *Send* button about 25 times."

I slid a calculator across my desk. "So you send and receive a total of 75 emails per day. Let's calculate your annual email volume: Multiply your 75 daily emails by 240, which is the number of work days per year. What do you get?"

Harold raised his eyebrows in wonder. "I process 18,000 messages per year? Wow."

"What else do you do 18,000 times a year?" I asked.

Harold paused, "I don't know… maybe breathe?"

"Right," I said, "next to life-sustaining activities, email may be what we do most."

"Ughhh," Harold groaned.

"We practically live for email and that's why we've got to do a better job of managing it. How much time do you think you spend on email each day, Harold?"

"I'm not sure, but I would guess at least two and a half hours."

"So it takes you 150 minutes to process 75 emails a day. That's an average of 2 minutes per email. Now multiply your 18,000 annual emails by 2 minutes to get the total number of minutes you spend on email each year."

Harold did the calculations and stared in disbelief, "36,000 minutes per year?"

I nodded and leaned forward. "Now divide by 60 minutes to get the total number of hours you spend on email each year."

Harold was even more dumbfounded. "600 hours per year? No wonder I can't get anything done!"

"Now divide by 8 hours to calculate the number of 8-hour workdays you spend on email each year."

"I spend 75 workdays per year on email? That's almost four continuous months of email a year! Can that be right?"

Harold was stunned. He did the calculation again and came up with the same number. Looking up he mused, "And this doesn't even include the email I do during holidays, vacations, and weekends."

I nodded and paused a moment to let it all sink in. "Let's cut to the chase, Harold. What percentage of the time that you spend on email is *wasted?*"

"Where do I start?" said Harold with a grimace. "People constantly send me long, unnecessary, and convoluted messages. I get copied on everything. *Reply-to-all* is out of control."

Harold paused to calm down and then blurted, "At least a third of the time I spend on email is poorly utilized or wasted!"

I nodded. "If you spend 75 days a year on email and a third of that time is wasted…"

Harold looked up in amazement. "Then I'm wasting 25 days a year on email?"

"That's more than a month of your career up in smoke each year. Using an average salary of $30 per hour, the cost of 25 wasted days is roughly $6,000 per worker each year or $6,000,000 for a company with 1,000 employees!" [4]

Slowly Harold reasoned, "So email isn't free at all. In fact, it's one of the *most* expensive things we do at Foster and Schrubb."

"And yet, you've received little or no guidance on how to manage it effectively," I guessed.

"That's true," said Harold quietly. At that moment, I noticed a change sweep over Harold's face. Suddenly, he looked more present and energetic.

Harold shot me a determined look. "Okay, Coach, teach me how to get my time back."

I grinned and said, "Okay. Now let's see — our goal is to reduce your annual email processing time by 20%. Because you spend 75 days a year on email, this equates to a savings of approximately 15 days. To achieve this goal, you'll need to change the way you think about email. Are you prepared to make some changes and leave your comfort zone, Harold?"

"I'll leave the planet to get back 15 days!" stated Harold firmly.

How Much Time Could You Save By Reducing Email by 20%?			
Emails Sent and Received Each Day	Annual Emails	Days Spent on Email	Days Saved with 20% Reduction
20	4,800	20	4
30	7,200	30	6
40	9,600	40	8
50	12,200	50	10
60	14,400	60	12
70	16,800	70	14
80	19,200	80	16
90	21,600	90	18
100	24,000	100	20

"Good," I smiled. "One more thing, Harold. How will you spend those 15 days?"

Harold thought for a moment, "Hmmmm. Not sure..."

I pushed a paper and pen across the table. "Take a moment and write down two important things you'd like to accomplish with 15 extra days over the next 12 months. Basically, 15 days a year equates to two and a half hours a week. Choose one personal and one professional goal. If you don't create a concrete plan for the time you'll save, you'll just wind up running harder and faster on the wheel."

"I'll default to email," acknowledged Harold. He thought for a moment and then wrote:

- *Personal: Take Kyle to karate two nights a week.*
- *Professional: Implement Accountability Training Program.*

Harold and I took a moment to discuss his goals. Apparently his 8-year-old son Kyle had been struggling with his grades and a certain bully at school. Kyle had expressed an interest in martial arts, but Harold, busy as always, hadn't followed up. As Harold discussed his son's struggles, I sensed that spending more time with him could make a big difference.

Harold also explained that Foster and Schrubb needed to develop a training program that promoted accountability. As the company had grown, lines of responsibility had become fuzzy. Many of Harold's co-workers failed to take ownership for key projects and decisions. Internal and external client satisfaction was dropping each quarter. Ironically, Harold had been tasked with creating an accountability program, but he had failed to follow through.

"I just couldn't find the time," he shrugged.

"I like your goals," I said. "They're realistic and attainable. Let me double-check something with you. Do they motivate you? Will you build them into your schedule in order to make them happen?"

"Absolutely," said Harold with conviction.

Reader Exercise: What personal and professional goals could you accomplish by joining the Hamster Revolution?

Hamster Revolution Goals	
Goal	**Type of Goal**
1.	Personal
2.	Professional

4

STRATEGY 1: REDUCE EMAIL VOLUME

Once Harold had chosen his goals, we began work on reducing his email volume.

"Okay, Harold, let's start with the simplest and most overlooked email reduction technique: *Send Less — Get Less*."

Harold shot me a look of disbelief, "How does sending less help? I mean, my problem is that *other* people send *me* too much email."

"At first glance, it doesn't seem like we have much control over email overload. But a closer look reveals something very different. Research shows that for every five emails you receive, three require a response.[5] This means that for every five emails we send, people send back three. I call this the boomerang effect. So if you eliminate just one out of every five outgoing emails, you'll begin to receive roughly 12% fewer emails."

"Plus I'd save the time it takes to create one in five outgoing emails," added Harold thoughtfully. "But, I'm pretty sure that most of my outgoing email is necessary."

"I agree," I said with a nod. "But *most* isn't all. I'd be willing to bet you a coffee that 20% of your email doesn't actually need to be sent."

"I'll take that bet," grinned Harold. "But I'm not sure how you're going to prove it."

"Let me give it a shot," I replied. "How do you feel as you process email each day?"

Harold thought for a moment. "Lately, I feel uptight. I have a knot in my stomach. I worry that I've missed some critical email buried deep in my inbox. Maybe that's why the unnecessary emails I get are so distracting and frustrating."

"Sounds stressful," I commented.

"It is. I usually have just a few minutes between meetings and I'm dashing off messages to colleagues on my PDA. I try not to miss anything urgent. Back at my desk, if I have some spare time, I usually dive in and try to delete or respond to as many emails as possible. At home, email is always on my mind. I'm constantly sneaking off to check messages and hammer out a few replies. When the kids catch me, boy, do they get mad!"

"It sounds kind of hectic and reactive."

Harold nodded. "With lots of interruptions. Your hamster wheel is a perfect analogy. Most of the time, I'm on auto-pilot: *Open–Read–Reply, Open–Read–Reply, Open–Read–Reply…*"

I nodded. "When we're stretched too thin, and primarily reacting to one interruption after another, we tend to send *me-mail*. Me-mail is all about rapidly clearing out *our* inboxes and pushing out lots of *our* information. It's all about me, me, me. Maybe that's why email has become an increasingly mindless process. We're losing track of what our recipients want and need. Vague, incomplete, and redundant messages are excellent examples of me-mail."

"Okay, but I don't think I'm sending me-mail it's mainly my co-workers," protested Harold.

"Initially, the vast majority of the professionals we've encountered feel just like you. But our research has revealed an interesting twist: 79% of the professionals we surveyed believe that their *co-workers* often overuse *Reply-to-all.*"

"You've got that right!" laughed Harold.

"...Only 13% believed that they, *themselves*, overuse *Reply-to-all.*"[6]

Harold stopped laughing and thought for a moment. "I guess when we're overwhelmed, it's easier to blame others versus taking responsibility. It's harder to ask, 'What's *my* role in creating this challenge?'"

I nodded. "And that's understandable. Just as new parents don't get an owner's manual, professionals receive very little coaching on email."

"Very little?" smirked Harold. "I haven't received any!"

"Have you ever *provided* email feedback to your colleagues?"

"Not really," admitted Harold with a shrug. "It's something we've never addressed at Foster and Schrubb. I guess we think, 'How tricky could email be?' We're supposed to be thinking about the bigger strategic things."

There was a long pause as something registered in Harold's mind. Slowly he reasoned, "Because we don't get any feedback, maybe we're all doing what we *think* works best instead of what actually *does* work best. Maybe we're missing a big opportunity to lighten our collective load."

"Exactly," I said, "In my experience, everyone has a different idea about what constitutes a necessary email. To reduce email volume, you need a simple, mutually agreed upon tool that clearly defines for everyone what should and shouldn't be sent."

"Oh, I love software," replied Harold. "Tell me I can download something to fix this mess."

I sighed. "It's not software, Harold. It's *headware*! It's a tool that sits up here." I tapped my forehead with my index finger, "In your mind, that helps you stop sending unnecessary email. This tool helps you to stop and ask three important questions before hitting *Send*."

Harold shot me a skeptical look. "Okay, what are these three magical *Ask Before You Send* questions?"

"Here you go," I said handing a small laminated card to Harold. "We call this the 1-2-3 Email Quantity Tool. It's going to save you a lot of time."

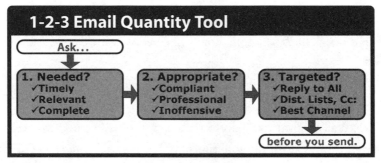

©2005 Cohesive Knowledge Solutions, Inc. All rights reserved. Copy only with CKS. All rights reserved. Copy only with permission.

Harold twitched his whiskers as he examined the simple diagram on the card, "How does this work?"

"Before hitting *Send*, ask: Is my email (1) Needed? (2) Appropriate? and (3) Targeted? Let's take them one at a time."

Question One is:

1. NEEDED?
(Does my busy recipient truly *need* this email to do his or her job?)

"If you take a moment to visualize your email recipient struggling through a typically busy day with a bunch of meetings and 100 emails in his inbox, you'll find yourself sending fewer and fewer unnecessary messages. You begin sending *we-mail* instead of me-mail. *We-mail* is information that is truly *needed* by the recipient in order to do his or her job. It's specific information for a specific purpose."

"I wish my colleagues sent more of that," laughed Harold, "Maybe I wouldn't be drowning in email."

"And perhaps," I offered gently, "Some of your colleagues wish that *you* considered their needs more carefully before hitting *Send*. Being judicious with email actually shows that you care for and respect your co-workers. Let me give you a few examples of email that isn't needed:

- **The FYI Light Email.** Many messages are sent because a sender suspects that *someone* on their team may *some*day be able to use *some* aspect of a particular piece of information. Many busy professionals find that they no longer have the time to read and store lengthy FYI light emails. In the future, tie every outgoing email to a *specific* business need.

- **The Trivial Thank You Email.** We all want to be polite. But trivial thank-you emails for routine tasks are becoming a pet peeve for a growing number of business people. It's one more unnecessary interruption in a workday already filled with interruptions. Has this ever happened to you? You're working on an important project that requires a lot of concentration...

your masterpiece… and ding, an email comes in. Someone is thanking you for sending the weekly report, which is something you do every week, and poof — you lose your train of thought?"

"Oh yeah, all the time," agreed Harold, "And sometimes, I never get back on track."

"Me either. In the future, in order to reduce email overload, the standard will be to reserve thank-you emails for extraordinary efforts. If you absolutely have to thank people frequently, consider showing your appreciation at your next meeting or as a part of a brief greeting in a more necessary email.

- **The Redundant Email**. When news breaks, we all want to pass it along. But too many times the same message is trumpeted around an organization by 17 different colleagues. Before sending an email, always consider whether someone else *has* or *will* be sending the same content.

- **The Incomplete Email**. In the age of wireless, handheld PDAs, it's tempting to send a series of partial replies to a single request. For example, sometimes we quickly send back a short acknowledgement or partial answer via PDA. Then, just a little while later, when we return to our computer, we send a second more robust reply. This is just one kind of incomplete email that drives recipients crazy because it takes time to piece together both replies. A better strategy is to wait until you're back at your desk and send one complete message to your recipient.

- **The Email Containing Searchable Info**. In the past, we understandably wanted to share every piece of useful information we encountered with our colleagues. Today, a growing percentage of that information is easily found on the Internet via keyword search and other web-based services.

For example, I no longer need people to email me directions because I can find them online in a flash. So before sending this type of info to my colleagues, I ask, 'Will my recipient store this piece of information or are they likely to search for it online?' If I think they'll search, I don't send it."

Harold was thinking. "I don't consider my recipients' needs that much. Sometimes I think, 'Hey, maybe Sue could do something with this' or 'Perhaps Ralph would get a kick out of that,' but I don't think about their busy lives, jammed inboxes, or the direct relevance of my message to their jobs."

"Would you be willing to take a look at some of the emails you've sent over the past few weeks?" I asked motioning toward Harold's laptop. He opened his laptop and pointed to his email.

"Have at it."

We spent the next 15 minutes filtering through Harold's last 30 emails.

"Okay, that one, that one, and that one," said Harold, pointing at his Sent Box with a shrug. "I'll admit that my colleagues didn't really need those."

Some of Harold's unnecessary emails were chatty and others contained outdated or redundant information.

He scratched his ear and took a deep breath. "So maybe I could cut back a little on unneeded email. But 3 out of 30 isn't bad, is it?"

"What do you think?" I asked with a smile. "That's a 10% reduction in outgoing email."

"Okay, I get it, email adds up. What's the next email reduction question?" asked Harold eagerly.

"*Ask Before You Send* Question Two is:

2. APPROPRIATE?
(Is this email compliant, professional, and inoffensive?)

"Eliminating inappropriate email is another way to drive down email volume while also reducing legal risk. Professionals often forget that email is *company property* that's stored forever and can be reviewed at anytime."

"Yeah, but who could possibly watch all the email streaming through Foster and Schrubb?" asked Harold. "Talk about a boring day job…"

"On a day to day basis, it's difficult. But IT departments are beginning to install software that can flag certain keywords and discussion topics. They can also retrieve any email you've ever sent in the event that a concern is raised."

"Well that's a scary thought."

"Well, you can't really blame them, Harold. As an HR pro, you know that companies have lost millions in legal penalties by failing to monitor inappropriate workplace behavior. The bottom line is that it's more important than ever to send email that's compliant, professional, and inoffensive."

"Could you be more specific?" asked Harold, "Getting sued is not on my to-do list."

"Sure:

> *A. Compliant.* Every company has an internal email policy. They also have to comply with various government laws. I'm sure that you don't knowingly send illegal email, but some messages fall into in a gray area. For example, you may be innocently asking about the legality of a particular action you're contemplating. I recommend conducting these kinds of communications face to

face rather than creating a permanent legal document that can be used in court.

B. Professional. Before sending a questionable email, ask yourself how you would feel if it appeared on the front page of a national newspaper. Would you look professional? If your email made an appearance on the evening news, would your company's stock price go up or down?"

"Wait a minute!" protested Harold. "If I send an email to my boss, how does it end up on the evening news?"

"Your boss could innocently forward it to someone she trusts. That person could send it on to 20 people. If one of those people has bad judgment or disagrees with the content of your email, then…"

"I'm sunk!" muttered Harold with a grim nod.

"I constantly remind myself that email is both *slippery and sticky*. It slithers and squirms into the oddest places and it *sticks* around forever. When it's unprofessional, it points a giant flashing spotlight back on you. That's why it makes sense to be more judicious and simply send less email. It's also important to make sure that outgoing email is completely…"

C. Inoffensive. There appear to be no censors or barriers in the email world. Although it's a business tool, it has a personal feel. We speak our minds and that's Okay, as long as we don't cross a certain kind of line. The problem is the line between offensive and inoffensive is in the eye of the beholder. Because we aren't present when our outgoing email is read and we don't know who it might be forwarded to, we have no real control over who reads our email. So my recommendation is to keep jokes, wise words of wisdom, and emotionally charged emails to an absolute minimum because…"

"Uh, oh," interrupted Harold, "no jokes?"

I smiled. "I'd be *very* careful about jokes. Let's say you forward a joke about blondes and it gets into the hands of someone who's blonde who works with you."

"Er, not good," admitted Harold, folding his paws over his chest.

"The scary thing about jokes is that the more funny and cutting they are, the more likely it is that they'll be forwarded. If you send an offensive joke to 20 people who each distribute it to 20 people who all forward it on to 20 more people, that joke will be viewed by more than 8,000 people. If it contains streaming video and takes 10 minutes to read, then you just spent 1,333 hours of company time."

"All by forwarding one stupid joke?" reflected Harold.

"Possibly," I said. "Or maybe you just sent it to a trusted friend whose child happened to look over his shoulder."

"Never thought of that," mused Harold.

"Also be aware that *wise words of wisdom* messages are often hoaxes. Be suspicious of any urgent email that asks you to forward a message to everyone in your address book. In many cases, these emails have been crafted by people with ulterior motives. Let me give you some examples:

- **Penny Brown:** An email containing a vague plea to help an abducted child named Penny Brown asks you to forward her information and picture to everyone you know. Key dates, facts, and legal information are oddly missing. Sadly, this distracts attention from real missing children.

- **Celebrity Rants:** A harshly worded email, supposedly written by a famous newsman, indicates that he's suddenly changed his long-held political views. Surprisingly, he blasts people that he's spent a lifetime supporting.

- **Get Rich Quick:** An attorney asks you to forward an email from Microsoft to every person you know. In a generous move, Bill Gates has offered to pay you $250 for each person on your forwarding list."

Harold laughed, "Ugh. I've got to admit that I fell for that last one. I'm still waiting for my big check!"

"You're not alone. Millions of people forward these kinds of emails each day. When you do it, you waste everyone's time while undercutting your own credibility."

"Is there some way to know if I'm being hoaxed?" asked Harold.

"Yes. There are some excellent fact-checking websites such as Snopes.com."

Harold nodded and made a note of the site.

"One last thought. From time to time you'll be tempted to send an angry email. You may have every right to be upset with someone. But I strongly recommend using the *24-Hour Rule*. Feel free to write your email — sometimes it's healthy to acknowledge your feelings, but wait one full day before hitting *Send*. Ninety-nine percent of the time, you'll cool down and replace your angry email with a more professional message."

"The 24-Hour Rule," stated Harold with a sigh, "That's good advice. I've noticed a growing number of edgy emails being sent by my team. When we're under pressure, things seem to escalate and etiquette goes out the window. Sometimes those emails cause a lot of hurt feelings and resentment. One of my co-workers just got demoted because of an angry message."

I nodded, "It can be a career-limiting move. The bottom line is that you can save yourself and your associates a lot of time by sending only *appropriate* email that's compliant, professional, and inoffensive."

"Got it," nodded Harold. "So the first two *Ask Before You Send* questions make perfect sense: Only send email that's 1. *Needed by your recipient* and 2. *Appropriate*, which means compliant, professional, and inoffensive. What's the last one?"

3. TARGETED?
(Is my email being sent to the right number of recipients through the best channel?)

"Targeting is the most effective way to cut email time. The opposite of targeting an email is spraying it everywhere. Targeting your email means that you decrease the use of the three most powerful email distribution tools: *Reply-to-all*, *Cc:*, and distribution lists. Let's take a look at each one.

Limit Use of *Reply-to-all*

Reply-to-all is by far the biggest source of email complaints.[7] When senders use this tool, they make the *assumption* that everyone on a particular distribution list wants to engage in a spontaneous, virtual group discussion."

"Let me guess, bad assumption?" snickered Harold.

"Right. Invariably, many *Reply-to-all* recipients don't have the time to carry on that kind of conversation. But once a *Reply-to-all* is sent, many recipients feel *compelled* to join the discussion. An email sent to 20 people can quickly morph into 100 confusing and disjointed emails just because one person hit *Reply-to-all* and four others felt obligated to chime in.

Harold looked sheepishly at his computer and mumbled, "I've been known to chime in from time to time," he squeaked.

"And sometimes it's perfectly appropriate," I said earnestly, "But whenever possible, try to cut back. Don't use *Reply-to-all* for minor discussion points, chatter, or trivial thank you messages. If you must respond to a widely distributed email, consider replying *only* to the original sender. If it's an involved situation that requires team input, perhaps arranging a *synchronous* discussion at an upcoming live meeting or teleconference would save time and have greater impact."

"Synchronous?" asked Harold.

"A synchronous communication is a discussion in which people respond back and forth to each other in real time. People hate *Reply-to-all* because it creates a disjointed *asynchronous* group conversation. When a group of people respond at different times, it becomes very hard to follow the flow of the discussion. By contrast, a synchronous conversation at a live team meeting allows for discussion, input, and a clear final decision."

"I see your point, but how can I stop my teammates from hitting *Reply-to-all?*"

"When sending an email to a broad distribution list, you and your colleagues can include this verbiage:

To save time, please reply only to me rather than hitting Reply-to-all."

"That could work," agreed Harold.

"A final tip is to use NRN in the subject line when sending an email for which **N**o **R**eply is **N**eeded. Some teams have begun to use NTN – **N**o **T**hanks **N**eeded. Just make sure that your entire team understands what NRN and NTN mean."

"So you're pre-empting replies by typing in three little letters in your subject line," said Harold thoughtfully. "That makes a lot of sense."

"Right. Now let's move on to the *Cc:* and Distribution list tools."

Limit Use of *Cc:* and Distribution Lists

"Ten years ago, when email was just beginning to ramp up, we were all thirsty to be copied on every message. Times have changed. With the information age upon us, it makes good business sense to become more judicious with *Cc:* and distribution lists. We must constantly remind ourselves that *less is more.*"

"Send Less — Get less," smiled Harold.

"Exactly. Remember to *Cc:* only those people who truly need to know. Complaints are growing from recipients who sense that they are being copied for the wrong reasons. Here are some examples:

- **Self-Promotion:** Copying a leader to show you're working hard or late
- **Manipulation:** Copying a colleague for political vs. business reasons
- **Humiliation:** Copying someone unnecessarily on an email in which the recipient is criticized or disciplined
- **Duplication:** Copying an associate to further document something that was already clearly documented

Overuse of *Cc:* can make a sender appear insecure, self-serving, and inefficient."

"Not a great way to build your professional image," quipped Harold.

"Finally, use distribution lists sparingly and create sub-distribution lists whenever possible. Ask to be taken off any distribution list that's no longer relevant to your job."

Harold glanced at his computer and gave me a guilty look. "I suppose you want to see if I've abused any of these targeting features?"

I nodded. As we combed through Harold's last 30 outgoing emails, we found four instances where Harold had used *Reply-to-all* when it really wasn't needed. He had also copied a number of people unnecessarily on several other emails.

"Four *Reply-to-alls* out of 30 emails isn't too bad," said Harold defensively.

"But Harold, you replied to an average of 15 people each time. That means that you actually created 60 additional unnecessary outgoing emails! Not to mention all the responses it triggered."

"Okay, Okay!" said Harold, raising his paws defensively, "I get your point: Minimize use of *Reply-to-all*, *Cc:*, and distribution lists."

"There is one more thing you can do," I said.

"Lay it on me, Coach."

"Carefully consider the communication channel through which you're sending your message. Before sending an email that's likely to result in a long back and forth discussion, carefully consider arranging a live, *synchronous* conversation instead."

"People should just pick up the phone!" exclaimed Harold.

"True," I said, "but keep in mind that 70% of all business phone calls[8] are now answered by machines."

"And now you're playing *asynchronous* telephone tag!" groaned Harold.

"Right. Too often we default to email because it's easy and we're in the habit of doing email. But the easiest channel isn't always the best channel. We need to invest more time in arranging discussions."

"So the key is to *schedule* a live conversation versus trying to get it all done via email or voice mail?" asked Harold.

"You bet. I also recommend exploring Instant Messaging (IM) as a way to conduct productive synchronous discussions. A person can reply to an instant message even when they're wrapped up in a phone call or meeting. They can respond by typing: "I'm in the middle of something, but I'll IM or call you back in 15 minutes. You can even set your IM profile to indicate if you're busy or available."

"So the key is to use IM to increase the amount of valuable synchronous dialogue versus frustrating asynchronous email threads and telephone tag?" asked Harold.

"Right."

"There's one small problem," said Harold sheepishly. "I have no idea how to use our corporate IM system."

"Some companies are holding back on IM. But if Foster and Schrubb offers IM, your IT team or a knowledgeable teammate can show you the ropes. Remember, IM should be used judiciously and only when you need a back and forth dialogue. When overused, IM simply creates more interruptions and busy work."

"I'll keep that in mind," said Harold. "There are so many ways to communicate these days," he mused, looking a little overwhelmed.

"You bet, Harold. That's why we constantly have to ask, 'Is this the *best channel* for my message?'"

I pointed at the 1-2-3 Email Quantity Tool: "Much of what we've discussed is summarized on this simple tool."

"It's simple," said Harold, looking carefully at the tool.

"Can you see yourself filtering out one of five outgoing emails with it?" I asked.

Harold studied the 1-2-3 diagram and taking a deep breath, nodded, "You know, I really think I can cut outgoing email by 20%. Guess I owe you a cup of coffee after all!"

"Then you'll save roughly 10 days a year. Later, I'll show you how to save an additional 5 days by improving email quality and coaching others. After we take a quick break, we'll dive into the quality and clarity of email. Ready?"

"Yes, sensei," Harold bowed respectfully with a glint in his eye. "Ready, willing, and able."

5

A TALE OF TWO EMAILS

After a quick break for coffee (Harold paid!), we began to explore ways to improve the quality of Harold's email. I handed Harold a printed email.

"I'd like you to read this email and stop when you understand the action required." I took out my stopwatch, "Ready, set, go!"

Harold quickly began reading the email, which was titled *One More Thing*.

....

To: Tiger Team National Distribution List
Cc: Ed Henry, Tyler Banks, Sheila Mehta, Cindy Wu
Attachments: NhddMtgNotes.doc, NatSls07.xls
Subject: One More Thing

Greetings.

I wanted to thank you all for your participation in last week's meetings. It was great seeing you all in sunny Florida. The information that you shared was really helpful and it will help us all to better service our customers in the future. In particular, Brenda's insights into the Cray account were really helpful. Her approach serves as a best practice for all of us. I am including the notes and action items for your review. As luck would have it, I need to ask some of you to do one more thing for me. Unfortunately, we need to take a look at our March numbers. We have been hearing that some of the numbers are being reported incorrectly. Other people are finding that the numbers are fine. If we want to get full credit for everything we do, we should jump on this immediately. In fact, we might also want to take a look at the February numbers to see if they also look right. This only applies to the East coast team. West coast numbers appear to be fine. So, please review the attached documents and let me know if you see any inconsistencies. I am also including some important information from the meeting including Brenda's best practices.

Oh yes, one more thing: We are looking to see if the March widget sales numbers are higher or lower than the February and January widget sales numbers. Generally speaking, they should be higher. If your numbers are lower, please call me at your earliest convenience.

Thanks again for all of your help last week. I think we got a lot accomplished in a very short period of time. Despite a somewhat cramped room and...let's just say, not the best food, we managed to execute like the champions that we are!

Andy

....

As Harold read, he sighed and shifted uncomfortably in his chair. The writer was communicating for a purpose, but the specific action was nowhere to be found.

"*Get to the point!*" Harold muttered impatiently. The message concluded with a vague request to send a report into headquarters. Harold looked up to indicate that at last, he was done. "Phew. I think this message is asking the reader to send in the February and March reports — but only if they see something funny in the numbers?"

"You don't sound very confident. Maybe you should read it again." I grinned, glancing at my stopwatch.

Harold groaned and buried his head in his paws. "Don't make me read it again. My hair hurts!"

"It took you 50 seconds to get through it. How'd that feel?"

"Frustrating," groaned Harold. "I get messages like this all the time — they seem to go on and on. Why can't people just get to the point?"

"We'll talk about that later, but first, read this second email and tell me what action is required." I handed another email to Harold, "Ready, set, go!"

Harold picked up the second email and instantly saw that it was much more structured than the first. The action requested was upfront and the key points in the body were neatly bulleted. By simply reading the title, he immediately understood the required action.

....

Subject: Action:
Please submit your district business plan to me by 5 PM 5/15.
Hey Tiger Team – Great meeting last week!

Action:
Follow guidelines below for business plan submission due 5/15.

Background:
• Remember to use specific and measurable goals.
• If you need to review instructions, go here: *www.mydistrictplan.net.*
• Be sure to stay within budget limits-$100k max. Sorry!

Close:
• Call me with questions and thanks for your help.
• Next meeting is 6/15: We'll discuss business plan implementation.

Thanks!
Angela Stevens
Regional Manager
Now Media
45 Power Team Blvd.
Innovation, CT 06437
203-987-6543
astevens@rm.com

....

"I need to send Angela my district business plan by May 15th."

"Seven seconds!" I announced, showing Harold the stopwatch, "How do the two messages compare?"

"The first message took 43 more seconds to read. Plus, I feel like it short-circuited my brain."

"How many of these long, drawn-out emails do you get a day?"

"At least five," replied Harold, "A couple people on our team think of email as a way to share their life story."

"The first email uses what we call a 'wall of words' style. There are no spaces or bullet points, just words, words, words, as far as your tired eyes can see. Five of these per day add up to 1200 confusing and time-consuming experiences a year. Poor email quality increases processing time and errors while confusing clients, but there is an even greater risk."

Harold looked up. "There is?"

"How do you feel about the person who wrote the long and confusing email?" I asked.

"He's completely wasting my time. He's trying to be nice, but he writes really frustrating email."

"What else?"

Harold thought out loud, "Well, he seems kind of scatterbrained and unprofessional."

"Not exactly the type of person that you'd rush to hire or collaborate with?"

"No," sighed Harold. His face brightened. "But I'd like to work with Angela. She's sharp as a tack and really seems to care about her team."

"What you're saying is that each email we send represents a tiny fraction of a *virtual resume* that we create over time. The clarity of your outgoing email now determines a considerable portion of your professional image. That's an important reason to strive for *absolute clarity* in every email you send."

Harold seemed to be reflecting on all the email he'd sent over the past few years. Perhaps he was thinking, "*Do I send messages like Andy or Angela?*" He looked back and forth between the two emails. "I guess I'd be a little nervous if I got placed on a project with Andy."

"Well, here's a surprise for you," I said with a wink. "Both writers are the same person!"

"What?" exclaimed Harold, studying both emails in disbelief, "No way! This Andy guy is an insufferable gasbag. He drones on and on."

"True. But these messages were written by the same person before and after joining the Hamster Revolution. Here's another twist. That *insufferable gasbag* is me!"

"Huh?" Harold stammered, looking embarrassed as I burst out laughing.

"I wrote both of those messages at different points in my career!" I explained with a smile.

"I'm sorry," said Harold, looking flustered. "You're Andy *and* Angela Stevens?"

"Yes. I changed the names to show how the Hamster Revolution can transform the quality of a person's email."

"No way!" exclaimed Harold. "I didn't mean…look, you're not a gasbag."

"Relax, Harold. I *was* a rambling gasbag before I learned how to create crisp, well-structured emails. The quality of my business writing probably improved *more* than 50% after joining the revolution. Now Harold, be honest: How do the emails you write compare to these two? Are you long-winded or clear and concise?"

"I was just wondering the same thing," said Harold sheepishly, "I'm probably somewhere in the middle."

"So, there's room for improvement?" I asked.

"Plenty," agreed Harold.

6

STRATEGY 2: IMPROVE
EMAIL QUALITY

"So, let's begin improving the quality and clarity of email," I said,
handing Harold another small, laminated card. "This is the
A-B-C Email Quality Tool and it's going to change the way you
write email."

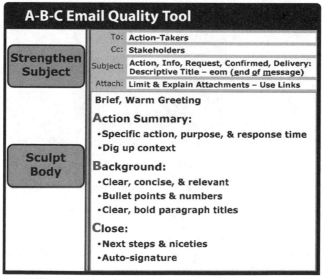

Harold studied the A-B-C tool, "Hey, this is neat. You've put the best practices in the exact place where they'd fall in an actual email."

I grinned, "Right. And we've also chunked the best practices for improving email quality into two important sections: *Strengthen the Subject* and *Sculpt the Body*." I rose to my feet. "In fact, these two insights are so often overlooked that I'd like you to stand for a special Hamster Revolution memorization ritual."

Harold stood up on his chair with a nervous smile.

Standing tall, I struck the classic bodybuilder's bicep pose. I bent my arms at the elbows and flexed as I said, "From now on, whenever we write an email we must *strengthen the subject*."

I then struck another famous bodybuilder pose known as "the crab." This entailed leaning forward and lowering my arms to waist level, making fists and bending my elbows slightly. I flexed with all my might as I turned from left and right, posing for an imaginary audience, "and *sculpt the body*! Now you try it, Harold."

"Strengthen the subject and sculpt the body," squeaked Harold, shyly looking around to see if anyone was watching. I got up and closed the door to make Harold feel more comfortable.

"Try it again, but make it louder this time — as if your life depends on it," I insisted with a look of mock exasperation. "Give it some umph, and don't forget to flex!"

This time Harold did the bicep pose and shouted, "*Strengthen the subject!*" He pulled his paws across his small torso in the crab pose, "*Sculpt the body!*" We both laughed at how ridiculous we looked. We repeated the exercise in unison for good measure.

"Good job," I said with a satisfied grin. "From now on you're going to pay special attention to creating emails with *strong* subject lines and *sculpted* bodies."

"Don't see how I could forget!" smiled Harold sitting down again.

Use Categories to Build Context

"Using simple subject *categories* before your title is a great way to begin strengthening the subject. I recommend using *Action, Info, Request, Confirmed,* and *Delivery.* These categories build context and rapid comprehension for your reader."

Harold nodded, "I'm familiar with *Action, Request,* and *Info,* but when do I use *Confirmed* and *Delivery?*"

"*Confirmed* helps your recipient know that you understand their request and have committed to a particular action. For example, if someone wants to know if you submitted an important proposal to a client, you might respond with an email titled:

Confirmed: Widget Proposal Submitted to Client X on 4/15

Delivery is used when you're responding to a specific request. It's your way of saying, 'I'm delivering exactly what you requested.' This creates instant context for the person who made the original request. For example:

Delivery: Completed Business Plan for Northeast District

"I like that. It leaves no room for misunderstandings," nodded Harold. "Hey, something just occurred to me. I get stressed when I'm unsure if people have actually done what they say they will. I wouldn't have so many nagging doubts if my co-workers used clear categories such as *Confirmed.*"

I smiled at Harold's growing insight, "Isn't it great? Better email yields peace of mind. And teams that use categories get more done because the purpose of each email is easily understood. Another benefit is that recipients can sort their inbox by email category. For example, they can sort their inbox to find all of the *Action* or *Request* emails, which is a great way to streamline workflow and focus on top priorities."

Descriptive Titles Eliminate Uncertainty

"The next key to *strengthening your subject* is to create a descriptive title. Vaguely worded titles are inefficient in two ways: They confuse the reader when they're first received and they also make it harder to relocate an email once it's been stored. Think about finding an email simply titled *Meeting*. How do you know which meeting?"

"Or my personal favorite — the blank subject line," laughed Harold.

"Mine is 'Hi there!' That really makes locating an email easy!" I said with a laugh.

"Unclear subject lines make it tough to find an email that's been filed. So, if you're sending out meeting notes to your team, instead of naming the email *Meeting Notes,* you could title it:

Delivery: Notes from Tiger Team Sales Meeting - 2PM 6/25 Rm. 213

"No confusion there," agreed Harold.

"Using specific dates, times, and places builds context and clarity for recipients. A specific and descriptive title makes email more concise because it forces you to stick with a clearly defined topic."

"Instead of rambling all over the world," moaned Harold.

"A final point on subject lines: Do you know how to *eom*?"

"I'm not really big on meditation," snickered Harold.

I laughed, "*Eom* isn't meditation. It stands for *end of message*. When someone types *eom* at the end of an email title, it means that the whole message is contained in the subject line. This saves time for both the sender and receiver."

"So I don't need to open an *eom* message because the title *is* the actual message?"

"You've got it, Harold."

Use Brief, Warm Greetings

"Before we learn how to sculpt the body of our emails, I thought we should discuss a common concern. Some people like to start off emails with a friendly comment or two to break the ice. Others feel that too much chitchat at the beginning of an email can confuse a message's true purpose. For example, someone may ask how you're doing or what your teammates have been up to lately."

"When the email is really about something completely different," noted Harold.

"Exactly. So, I recommend using a concise salutation such as 'Hi Harold,' plus a *brief but warm* statement at the beginning of my messages. Try to keep the whole greeting to one line with fewer than eight words. Here are a few examples:

Hi Kelly– Nice job on the Baker account.

Hi Mark – Thanks for sending the sales report.

Hey Team – Great meeting last week.

Harold nodded, "These greetings satisfy both the people who want to start an email with a kind word and those who want to get right to the point. It's the best of both worlds."

Use A-B-C to Sculpt the Body

"Now that we've learned how to *strengthen the subject* of your emails, let's look at how you can *sculpt the body* using the A-B-C method. A-B-C is a structure that puts the right information in the right place in the body of every email you send. It increases the *readability* of each message, which helps both the sender and recipient accomplish more. A-B-C can also be used for voice mail, letters, and other communications."

I pointed to the A-B-C tool, "The key is to break the body of your message into three distinct sections:

- **A**ction Summary

- **B**ackground

- **C**lose

Action Summary: An Action Summary is a single sentence that summarizes the specific action, purpose, or key point of your email. Nothing is more frustrating than having to read several paragraphs to understand why a particular email was sent."

"It's really time-consuming," said Harold.

"That's another reason why a powerful Action Summary is becoming more and more critical. A clear Action Summary makes it possible for the reader to quickly respond to an email without having to sift through the entire message or a long email thread. The Action Summary eliminates uncertainty, which allows you to relax your mind and focus on the actions you need to take."

Harold seemed pensive.

"You look thoughtful, Harold. What's up?"

"This is kind of a revelation for me. If all my incoming email became clear and concise, I could focus more on taking action versus figuring out what the other person is trying to convey. I'd accomplish more with a lot less stress."

"Exactly, and for longer emails, the Action Summary is a helpful introduction to the content that will follow. For shorter emails, the Action Summary can be the entire email. In either case, it's important for the Action Summary to provide a healthy dose of clarity and context to the reader."

Dig Up the Context for Short Replies

"In the age of PDAs and text messaging, vague or brief replies are a common cause of confusion. For example, someone might write 'Sounds good.' 'I'm in,' or 'I'm all over it' in response to an email. This kind of reply can cause confusion, especially if the email is a reply to a longer thread in which multiple topics are discussed. In many cases, the short reply is clear to the sender, who knows what he or she's trying to say, but confusing to the recipient. A far better approach is to *dig up* the context of the email thread and jam it into the Action Summary. This saves a great deal of mental energy for the recipient who may be processing 50 or more incoming emails each day. Here are some examples."

Vague Reply	Action Summary Reply
Sounds good.	Agreed: I will shorten the proposal to four pages and add a graph on glazed donut sales by 5 PM 4/15.
I'm in.	Confirmed: I will attend the 4/15 Sales Meeting and yes, I will bring the glazed donuts and coffee.
I'm all over it.	Final Decision: Manufacturing will decrease the production of glazed donuts by 25% starting on 4/15.

Harold nodded, "You're making things absolutely clear right from the start."

"Digging up the context is an easy way to speed communications and improve your professional image. It also increases the odds that people will act on the emails you send."

"This is really helpful," said Harold. He held up a paw as something crossed his mind. "Wait a minute. If our sales team started using action summaries, their emails would be easier to read and understand. Do you think it might impact sales?"

"Absolutely, Harold. Your clients are just as overloaded by email as you. I'm sure they'd appreciate it if your sales team began sending clearer and more easily understood emails. It could definitely increase revenue for Foster and Schrubb. Now let's look at the next section of the A-B-C message structure. **B** stands for Background.

Background section: Here is the body of your message. This is the place where a little sculpting goes a long way. In this section, resist the urge to simply write out all your thoughts in a long, unstructured *wall of words* format. Instead, take a moment to sort and hone your ideas. Then place them in a logical order. Use space to clearly separate one idea from the next, but also try to limit your email to a single screen page. Here are some additional background thoughts:

- **Chunk Your Key Points.** Bullet points are a welcome relief for tired eyes. They're also the easiest way to chunk your key points. If you have more than five sentences in a bullet point section or paragraph, consider creating a bold, underlined heading summary. If you're describing a sequential task or process, use numbers rather than bullets.

- **Define and Limit Attachments**. If your email has attachments, clearly define the purpose of each attachment in the Background section. If you have a long attachment, let the reader know the page and paragraph where the key point can be found. It's a good idea to minimize the total number of attachments you send and to substitute links whenever possible. Links reduce the total number of document versions in circulation while also reducing the amount of data that your IT department needs to back up each day.

- **Keep Emails to Execs Concise**. Executives appreciate crisp communications that get right to the point. Make sure that you aren't including unnecessary and distracting background information when emailing high-level colleagues."

"Some execs tell me that given the sheer volume of email they receive, they're often forced to delete messages that aren't immediately crystal clear," said Harold.

Close section: The end of your email is a great place for:

- **Extensive Niceties**. While it's fine to offer a brief, warm greeting at the outset of your email, it can be distracting when several sentences of chitchat precede an important action request. Placing extended niceties, chitchat, or kudos at the end of your email keeps these sentiments from getting in the way of your core point.

- **Next Steps**. In some emails, it's helpful to provide a description of related events that are likely to happen in the future. These aren't actions but rather a general ideas connects the current email with future initiatives.

- **Auto-signature.** A well-crafted auto-signature provides important contextual information. It identifies who you are and what you do. A strong auto-signature also projects a more professional image while providing alternative ways for people to get in touch with you via phone, IM, fax, or snail mail."

"A-B-C," mused Harold, "Action, Background, Close… that's easy to remember."

"Perfect. Now let's combine our first two Hamster Revolution strategies," I said, handing Harold a 4" x 6" tent card featuring the 1-2-3 and A-B-C tools on the front. "Later, we'll place Strategies 3 and 4 on the back of this card and you'll have one simple desktop aid for the entire Hamster Revolution."

"Cool," murmured Harold as he studied it carefully. "I can put this by my computer and refer to it when I'm processing email."

"And eventually it will become second nature to reduce email quantity while improving email quality."

"And so the revolution spreads," whispered Harold with a wicked grin.

"Any final questions on the quality of email?" I asked.

"How casual should an email be?" Harold asked, "Some people at work seem to be abandoning punctuation and grammar altogether."

I nodded, "It's an outgrowth of our busy schedules and the fact that a lot of people are communicating with PDAs and cell phone text messaging. In your personal life, it's not a big deal to be a bit relaxed with grammar. I don't use the A-B-C structure or get stressed about grammar when I'm letting my mom know how the kids are doing. But at work, email etiquette is important."

"Got it," said Harold. "Any more email etiquette advice?"

"Sure. Here are a few email etiquette best practices to keep in mind:

- ALL CAPS IS CONSIDERED SHOUTING. So is overpunctuating!!!!!

- When you don't use caps appropriate punctuation or proper grammar its a lot harder to understand what ur trying to say.

- Text messaging abbreviations r confusing 2 ur co-workers.

- Avoid using emoticons that others may not understand. ;o)

- Join the AAAAA (American Association Against Acronym Abuse). Explain acronyms before using them.

- Be sure to check your spelling and grammar before sending. Most email programs allow you to do this automatically. Outlook® users can simply hit the F7 key.

- Keep communications clear and concise when messaging to people who speak a different primary language. Also limit use of expressions unique to one culture such as 'We're on a roll!' when addressing a multicultural audience.

"Poor email etiquette screams out me-mail," said Harold, raising his arms high. "Thanks, Coach!"

"You're welcome, Harold. Now that we've covered email quantity and quality, our third and final topic for today is Info-Coaching. Would you like to learn how to get your colleagues to send you clear, concise, and actionable email?"

"And less of it?" asked Harold hopefully.

"Much less," I replied.

"Bring it on," said Harold.

7

STRATEGY 3: INFO-COACHING SUSTAINS RESULTS

Harold leaned forward in his chair. This was the moment he'd been waiting for.

"So what about everyone else?" he asked eagerly, "How do I get *others* to send me better email? How do I get *them* to join the revolution?"

"The key is to become an effective Info-Coach."

"How do I do that? I'm pretty new at this."

"I understand how you feel. After all, Info-Coaching is a new concept. Only 15% of the professionals we surveyed receive regular coaching on information-management related tasks like email. Yet 89% believed that coaching could improve the value of email."[9]

"Why is it so rare?" asked Harold.

"There are actually three interrelated challenges, Harold.

1. **Defensiveness:** Some professionals feel embarrassed or annoyed when coached on a common task like email. Sensing this, many simply refrain from coaching.

2. **Lack of Execution:** When people *do* learn a best practice or guideline, they often fail to implement it for very long because there is no tool or standard to remind them.

3. **Lack of Knowledge:** Without training or experience, professionals have no idea how to provide Info-Coaching.

"So how do you change all that?" asked Harold.

"With this." I handed Harold another small laminated card.

"Let me guess, another tool?" chuckled Harold.

"Right," I smiled. "This is the Hamster Revolution Info-Coaching Tool. It will help you evolve into a successful Info-Coach over the next few weeks. This tool outlines three simple steps you can take to address the three challenges I just mentioned."

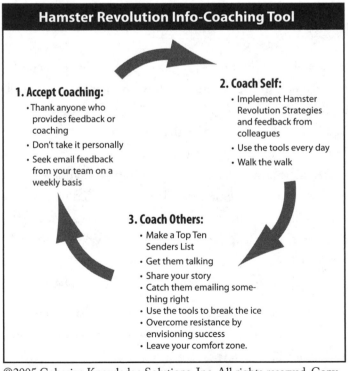

Harold examined the Info-Coaching Tool. "So first I've got to accept coaching from others?"

"Exactly. It can be frustrating and embarrassing to receive coaching on a common task like email. Instead of becoming defensive, *thank* the person providing the coaching and ask for more feedback."

"It was a bit uncomfortable looking at my email inbox with you today," said Harold.

"But did it help?"

"You bet."

"Being receptive to coaching gives you credibility as you begin to provide it to others."

"I'll definitely start asking for feedback," said Harold glancing down at the Info-Coaching Tool. "And I totally *get* the second Info-Coaching step: Coach Self. *Walking the walk* really makes sense. I've got to implement everything I've learned, so that I can lead by example."

"Right. It's hard to ask others to change when you have not."

"So I combine the 1-2-3 and A-B-C Tool insights with the feedback I get from my colleagues and make sure that I put everything into practice."

"Right. Now you've set the stage for step three, the most rewarding and challenging aspect of Info-Coaching — Coach Others. We're going to spend the rest of our time today discussing this topic. Ready to leave your comfort zone, Harold?"

"Yes, but I'm not exactly sure where to begin."

"Let's start with the results we hope to achieve. Visualize what it would be like if everyone at Foster and Schrubb responded to your incredible Info-Coaching and joined the Hamster Revolution."

Harold leaned back in his chair and put his paws behind his head. He squinted as if he was trying to peer into the future. "The entire company would get a lot more done. Our inboxes wouldn't be overflowing with unnecessary, confusing messages from colleagues. The email that we'd get would be clear, concise, and actionable. I think everyone would feel calmer and more focused."

"Okay, Harold, use that powerful vision to motivate yourself. That's where Info-Coaching can take you."

"It *would* be amazing," mused Harold. "But…"

I raised my eyebrows, "But what?"

"Beyond the concept of Send Less — Get Less, how on earth can I control what other people do with email?"

I looked at Harold's computer again. "Perhaps you have more control than you think. Roughly what percentage of your email comes from people you consider to be *teammates*?"

Harold looked at his inbox. "Well, I'm on a bunch of teams: the HR team, the Organizational Effectiveness team, and several small project teams. It looks like 60% of my email comes from people I consider to be teammates."

"Do you give those people feedback on general business issues?"

Harold nodded, "Of course. We're big on feedback at Foster and Schrubb. It's one of the cornerstones of our leadership model."

"…except when it comes to email?"

Harold was pensive. "I get your point. If most of our email comes from teammates, why shouldn't we provide feedback on that, too?"

"I believe in the 80–20 rule, Harold. I'll bet a large percentage of your email comes from a small subset of people — many of whom are your teammates. We need to target our Info-Coaching to the ones who send us the most. Who are your top ten email senders, Harold?"

Harold shot me a look that said, "*I have no idea.*" I motioned for him to look at his computer. He thought for a moment and then sorted his email inbox by sender. Instantly, he could tell who was sending him the most email. He jotted the names down on a piece of paper.

"Now write one coaching suggestion for each person on your list. Use the 1-2-3 and A-B-C Email Tools as your guide."

Harold reviewed the emails that had recently been sent by his teammates and compiled his list of people and suggestions. When he was done, he slid his list across the desk to me.

"Now you know *who* needs *what* kind of Info-Coaching."

Harold's Top Ten Email Coaching List	
Name	**1 Area of Improvement**
1. Dhara Mehta	FYI emails
2. Roger Fields	Reply-to-all
3. Janet Edwards	Wall of words
4. Mary Wong	Confusing background
5. Enos Knitz	No caps!
6. Marsha Waters	Reply-to-all
7. Sales Team (Dave A.)	Strength subject-ABC
8. Jon Fripp	CYA, FYI, Reply-to-all
9. Carol Schultz	Incomplete PDA emails
10. Ali Nanda	ABC

"But aren't these people going to be defensive like you said?" asked Harold.

"Isn't that true of every kind of coaching, Harold? At first it's awkward, but what's the alternative? Not getting your needs met? Ignoring an efficiency problem? The time for action is now. Email volume is rising at a compounded rate of 14.6% per year."[10]

"Time to leave my comfort zone," said Harold firmly.

"Right. Tell me something, Harold. How do you feel when someone directly states their needs?"

"It's refreshing. I immediately understand how I can help them."

"Can you see the benefit in sharing your email-related needs with colleagues? Wouldn't that be a gift of sorts?"

"It would," said Harold tentatively. "It could help them get more done and improve their professional image."

"Exactly. So tell me about some of the people on your Top Ten Email Senders List?"

Harold nodded, "Okay, let's start with the toughest person on my list: my boss, Dhara Mehta. She's a great leader, but she sends out a ton of FYI emails every day. No one has the time to read them all. Sometimes she loads these emails up with long attachments. I can't just walk in and tell my boss to knock it off."

I thought for a moment. "It can be awkward to coach a supervisor or executive. But in many cases, they and their assistants are the ones sending email to the largest number of people."

"True," agreed Harold.

"What price does Dhara pay for *not* knowing how frustrating her emails can be?"

"Well, she's missing a chance to make us more productive. She's losing a chance to address an issue that's causing frustration for her team." Harold scratched his chin, "Maybe I could share the 1-2-3 and A-B-C tools with her but I'm still a little nervous. After all, she's my boss."

"Hmm," I thought for a moment. "Here's a strategy for the next team meeting attended by Dhara. What if you requested 10 minutes on the agenda for an email efficiency discussion? Show the 1-2-3 and A-B-C Email Tools to the team and explain how it has helped you become more effective. Good leaders like Dhara will often ask if you have any feedback for her. If she does, that may be an opportunity to bring up the FYI light emails. Another option is to discuss it offline."

"Hmmm," said Harold. "She usually does ask for feedback at meetings so that might just work. And my whole team would see this as away to be more productive."

"Who else is on your Top Ten Email Senders List?"

"Roger Fields reports to me and he's very chatty on email. He hits that *Reply-to-all* more than anyone on our team. I could probably use a more direct approach with him."

I nodded. "I use the direct approach whenever possible. However, I'd recommend first telling him about your experience with the Hamster Revolution and asking for feedback on how you're doing with email. You might learn something about your own messaging habits. Then, in a one-on-one setting, provide him with direct feedback on how *Reply-to-all* impacts productivity. Ask him to consider replying *only* to the primary sender, which in many cases is probably you."

"That might work with Roger, but I'm not so sure about some of HR's internal clients," said Harold. "For example, I've been assigned to service the Sales Management Team and those people are tough. They're a really talented, hard-driving bunch, but they hate spending time on anything that doesn't relate directly to closing business deals."

"What kind of Info-Coaching do they need?" I asked.

"Well, they often send really vague email requests from their wireless PDAs. Their subject lines are often single words such as *meeting* or *FYI*. It leads to a lot of misunderstandings. The sales team is led by a VP named Dave Anderson and we've knocked heads a few times over the years. He's a real driver and a bit defensive."

I thought for a moment,."I always try to keep two things in mind when working with sales teams: (1) They're paid to have a laser-like focus on their clients' needs and (2) They're usually frustrated by administrative burdens that reduce face time with customers."

Harold's face brightened, "So maybe I should frame the discussion around increasing sales and decreasing admin."

"And because you mentioned that Dave is a bit defensive, first explain an email skill that you're working on. Bring the 1-2-3 and A-B-C Email Tools and explain how they've helped you. Defensive people relax when they realize they're not being singled out. Maybe it would help to have a set of tools for each member of the Sales team? You can find them at hamsterrevolution.com."

"Great. I could show how the email tools help everyone create more clear and professional looking email, the kind of email that clients and co-workers really like to get. You know, we've never trained our sales people to create more professional and persuasive looking email."

"…which could ultimately boost sales! We've been helping organizations to do just that. Many sales people needlessly alienate clients with poorly written emails. I have a collection of confusing ones that various vendors have sent over the years. We've contacted many of these companies. Some have asked us to help them create more client-friendly email."

"I hope Foster and Shrubb isn't in your 'collection,'" said Harold, using his paws to make air quotes, "But it wouldn't surprise me if we were. Most of our sales communications flow through email these days."

"And it isn't just Sales that could benefit from improved email skills." I said, "Every team at Foster and Schrubb has its own special reason to join the Hamster Revolution:

- **Information Technology:** IT departments want to reduce email overload so that they can reduce the cost of backing up unnecessary email and attachments. They also field a lot of complaints about email that have more to do with user behavior than with technology problems.

- **Knowledge Management:** Knowledge Management teams are often tasked with improving the net value of information streaming through their organization. Email, the vehicle through which most of our information flows, is a logical place to start.

- **R&D:** Research teams are packed with brilliant scientists and researchers. Although they have great ideas, they often struggle to communicate in a clear and succinct manner. As a result, fantastic ideas are often overlooked or misunderstood.

- **Legal:** Corporate attorneys understand that expensive lawsuits often result from poorly conceived or inappropriate emails. Another legal issue is that lawyers often write long and complex emails that very few recipients understand, which in turn can lead to misunderstandings that result in costly legal proceedings.

- **Project Management:** Colleagues who are responsible for managing critical projects often send and receive an unusually large amount of email. Improving the value of email helps projects stay on track.

- **Executives:** Execs have the challenging task of rolling out major initiatives to large groups of employees. Execution is impossible without clearly communicated plans, action steps, and progress updates. Talented execs often see solid initiatives undermined by poorly written emails."

"And I can certainly see how this will help HR," said Harold. "Almost every day, we communicate important information across the entire organization. If we crafted better emails, I think we'd get a better response and be more valued by the rest of the company."

I nodded, "And Info-Coaching is the key to spreading the Hamster Revolution to all the departments we just discussed. Here's a final Info-Coaching tip. Once you're starting to see results, make sure that you *catch people emailing something right*. For example, you can print out copies of a well-written message and bring it to your next team meeting. Show people what *great* looks like and they'll begin creating great email. You can also include a positive comment in a reply to a well-structured message or discuss email skills at a performance review. If you remain passionate, you will find that Info-Coaching spreads and sustains the Hamster Revolution."

"And in the end, everyone wins," said Harold.

I smiled. "And keep in mind that Info-Coaching is an ongoing process. That's why it's a circular tool. As long as you continually Accept Coaching, Coach Yourself, and Coach Others, you'll find yourself sending *and* receiving less email."

"And the email that I get will be more clear and easier to process," added Harold.

"Exactly."

Harold glanced at his watch and realized that our time was up. "Time to put *Operation Reclaim Harold's Life* into action," he said with confidence. "One small step for the Hamster Revolution — one giant step for me!" Harold packed up his computer and hopped off his chair. Together, we walked to the elevator in the lobby.

"Remember, Harold, change isn't easy for some folks. You're bound to have a few setbacks along the way. We've covered a lot today, but there's more to learn. So feel free to call or IM me whenever you run into trouble. Let's meet at *your* office the same time next week to cover the fourth Hamster Revolution Strategy: effectively filing and finding information. That way, we can see exactly how you're organizing your information."

"I wouldn't call it organizing, more like frantically stuffing email into a bunch of folders or simply letting it accumulate into a mountain in my inbox," said Harold with a grin.

In closing, I asked Harold to complete one homework assignment for me. I wanted him to come up with a rough estimate of how many emails and documents he was storing. As Harold headed out the door, I asked him if the meeting was a good use of his time and if it met his expectations.

Harold reflected for a moment. "Absolutely. I have to admit that it's given me hope. I'm ready to give it a try. Thanks, Coach."

Reader Exercise: Make your own Top Ten Email Senders List. What coaching can you provide? What strengths can you recognize?

List Your Top Ten Email Senders		
Name	1 Area of Improvement	1 Area of Strength
1.		
2.		
3.		
4.		
5.		
6.		
7.		
8.		
9.		
10.		

8

HELP! IT'S NOT
SO EASY!

Later in the week, Harold pinged me via IM. I was finishing up a meeting with a client.

Harold: Coach, you there?

Info-Coach: Hi. On phone-Give me 2 mins.

Two minutes later...

Info-Coach: Okay, I'm back. Hey – You learned how to IM. Congrats!

Harold: Thanks. I'm waiting for the sales team meeting to start. I didn't want this conversation to be overheard, so I'm using IM.

Info-Coach: I'm impressed, perfect application for IM. What's up?

Harold: This is the HR-Sales meeting. Remember, the sales team sends those vague, confusing emails from their PDAs.

Info-Coach: Yes. I remember.

Harold: I'm a bit nervous. I asked for time on the agenda to discuss email and Dave Anderson was pretty skeptical. He cut the agenda time I reserved down to 5 minutes and said, "*Email isn't a problem here.*"

Info-Coach: Okay.

Harold: Well, what if they think my presentation is a waste of time?

Info-Coach: A waste of time? 15 days for you and them? More sales + less admin = more life.

Harold: Yeah, Yeah. I get it. I still don't know how to start. The meeting begins in 3 minutes. They're filing in already. They look grumpy. Maybe they didn't hit their sales quota. I think I'm gonna barf.

Info-Coach: Relax and take a deep breath. Focus. First, get them talking.

Harold: Okay, I'm breathing again... oxygen returning to brain. OK, now what?

Info-Coach: Ask them what bugs them most about email.

Harold: That's it? That's your big advice? How much am I paying you? Ha, ha.

Info-Coach: Just try it. When they start to vent, explain that you've learned a new system that addresses lots of their frustrations. Ask if they'd be interested in seeing it. When they say yes, hand out the 1-2-3 and A-B-C Email Tools. Did you bring them?

Harold: Yes. Okay. Anything else?

Info-Coach: Ask for feedback on your own email first. Show them that you're willing to listen, learn, and improve.

Harold: Great idea. I hope they catch the spirit.

Info-Coach: They will. You can also send them to the hamsterrevolution.com for more info. There are helpful online exercises, efficiency tips, and . . .

Harold: That sounds like shameless self-promotion.

Info-Coach: Perhaps, but the site does have lots of helpful and free info.

Harold: Okay. Gotta go. Meeting starting.

Info-Coach: Call me at 2 PM. I'll keep my phone line open.

Harold: Got it. Out.

Info-Coach: Let them vent. Listen first.

Harold: What part of "Out" don't you understand? Ha, Ha.

At 2 PM the phone rang. It was Harold and he was excited. "It worked! I got them venting and soon everyone was joining in."

"Perfect. What did you cover?"

"There were so many concerns raised. It was really amazing. They have more issues with email than I do. Even Dave had some complaints about angry messaging. He loved the 24-Hour Rule."

"Dave? The guy who almost cut you out of the agenda?"

"Two minutes into the session, everyone was pointing out what frustrated them about email. A couple top sales managers repeatedly mentioned it was reducing face time with clients. Dave loosened up after that."

"Great. Did you ask them for feedback on your email?"

"Didn't have to. They picked apart a few of my recent emails on the spot. To be honest, they were right. The whole HR team tends to be a bit verbose. I showed them the tools and the website. They seemed really interested in learning more about the Hamster Revolution."

"What were the specific outcomes of the meeting?"

"Everyone committed to talking to their people about the Send Less — Get Less principle in order to reduce email volume. The sales managers are going to help their people to *strengthen the subject* and *sculpt the body* of each email they send. They're interested in learning more about Info-Coaching and team training. Dave seemed really pleased with the discussion."

"They got it," I said with relief. "Good job, Harold."

"It was the last thing they wanted to fix and now it's at a top priority," crowed Harold.

"And how do you feel?"

"Great. I feel like we accomplished something important for one of HR's hardest-to-please internal clients, something we should have addressed a long time ago. This brought our teams together to tackle a common enemy and that's a powerful thing."

"Remember to catch Dave and other members of the Sales team *emailing something right* in the next couple of weeks. I'll see you in a few days."

9

HAROLD'S PROGRESS CHECK

Our next meeting had been strategically scheduled to occur at Harold's office in the Foster and Schrubb HQ building. Janet, Harold's administrative assistant, greeted me with a big smile as I stepped off the elevator. She leaned over and whispered, "So you're the one who's helping Harold with his email?"

"I am," I said with a smile.

"Well, just between you and me, it's working."

"What's working?"

"The Hamster Revolution."

"You know about the Hamster Revolution?"

"Of course! That's all Harold's talked about for the past week."

"Has anything changed as a result?" I asked.

"It's made my job a lot easier. I don't manage Harold's inbox, but we do send each other a lot of email. He's suddenly sending a lot less to everyone and the email he does send is much easier to understand. And one other thing…"

Janet stopped walking and whispered, "He seems a little more like his old self, if you know what I mean."

"In what way?" I asked leaning forward.

"Well you know," said Janet cautiously, "in his overall, er, demeanor."

"Since you brought it up, just how long has Harold been a ham…?"

"Ahem!" We both looked up and saw Harold smiling as he walked down the hall toward us holding two cups of coffee. He was definitely still a hamster, but a happier and more relaxed hamster than when we first met.

"Well here's Mr. Sunshine himself!" laughed Janet nervously.

"Thanks for walking me in, Janet. I'm glad things are going well," I said with a smile.

Harold thanked Janet and handed me a coffee. "Here's my office, Coach," he said, "Come on in."

It was a small, well-furnished office that featured a picturesque view of the city. Harold had a beautiful wooden desk with a few piles of paper on it. His leather chair had a couple of phone books stacked on it so that he could work more comfortably. I noticed that he had placed the email productivity tools right next to his computer.

"Before we talk about how you file and find your information, I'd like to know how things are going with the email insights we discussed last week."

Harold sat down at his desk and motioned for me to take a seat.

"I let everyone know that I'd joined up," he beamed, "and that got a whole bunch of email Info-Coaching conversations rolling. It was tough and a little awkward at first. I really did feel anxious. I simply explained how I was trying to change my email habits and that seemed to interest a lot of people. At first people laughed at the whole hamster thing but then I told them about saving 15 days a year."

"That got their attention?" I interjected.

"It did. My boss Dhara and Janet were a bit defensive at first. I took your advice and asked for feedback on my email. They gave me some great coaching and then allowed me to provide coaching to them. Apparently, some of my emails weren't as clear as I'd originally thought. Dhara's definitely sending fewer of those FYI emails that were slowing me down."

"And you've been following up with other people on your Top Ten Senders List?"

"Yes and I took it one step further. I added a little tag line at the end of my outgoing emails."

"What does it say?" I asked.

"Sick of Email Overload? Join the Revolution! Ask me how."

"Wow. Great idea, Harold."

"And people can't help but ask, 'What in the world are you talking about?'"

"And once the conversation starts…"

"…the revolution spreads!" laughed Harold. "I'm definitely saving more than 30 minutes a day thanks to the Hamster Revolution. That's two and a half hours a week or 15 days a year. It's weird, I'm suddenly able to focus on what matters most without feeling so harried."

"You're making great progress, Harold."

"Thanks, but it gets even better. Kyle and I talked about karate and we're going to build it into our schedule. I'm also starting to put my ideas together for the Accountability Project. It's long overdue."

I smiled and we sat for a moment without talking.

Harold said, "I can't thank you enough, Coach. I've still got a long way to go. But already, I'm a bit of a zealot; I really love sharing the Hamster Revolution strategies with people. I've also come to understand that not everyone will join and that's OK, too."

I smiled, "You've accomplished a great deal. Our work is more than halfway done. Now it's time to focus on the way you file and find your info. Are you ready for the fourth Hamster Revolution Strategy?"

Harold looked nervous but excited. "Sure. But this won't be pretty. My files are a mess."

10

CHAOS IN INFO-LAND

My files are a mess! I'd heard this confession a thousand times. This was the big, dirty secret of the information age. In fact, 78% of the 2,000+ professionals we'd surveyed reported that they *often* find it time-consuming and frustrating to locate email and documents.[11]

"Harold, has anyone ever helped you organize your files?" I asked.

"Not really. A few colleagues have given some advice, but it hasn't helped. By the way, I completed that homework assignment."

"Great. So how many emails and documents are stored on your computer?"

"Over 8,000!" said Harold, "I'm amazed that I've accumulated so much stuff."

"That's like managing a small town library without any training," I noted. "Mind if I move my chair so I can see your computer screen?"

"Not at all," said Harold.

I picked up my chair and walked around Harold's desk so that we could both look at his computer at the same time. Together we explored the various places where he stored his information.

Harold had email, documents, and links stored in several places:

- Email Inbox: 454 emails.

- Email Storage Folders: 57 primary email folders jammed with over 5,000 emails. A few of the folders had sub-folders, but most were filled with hundreds of emails.

- Document Storage: 45 document folders packed with several thousand documents and attachments.

- Links: 211 links stored in one long list in *My Favorites.*

Harold got up and pointed to his filing cabinet. "And things aren't much better in here. I call this the Blue Monster because it eats up all my hard copy documents."

I stood and walked over to Harold's filing cabinet, which was about 10 feet from his desk. Its four drawers were jammed with over a hundred folders in a rough kind of alphabetical order. Some of the folder names matched his computer files, but many were different. He had used different colored folders and various types of pens and markers for his labels. There was a lot of variation.

"Things just seem to vaporize," said Harold with a vacant look in his eyes. We walked back to our chairs and sat down.

"You're not alone, Harold. Remarkably, half of all initial attempts to locate information are unsuccessful. That's a lot of wasted time and energy. The time spent searching for lost information costs companies like Foster and Schrubb $5,000 per employee each year. For a company like yours with over 8,000 employees, that's $40 million a year in wasted time.[12] Even in this era of powerful desktop search tools, many people feel oddly *disconnected* from their information."

"That's how I feel," stated Harold flatly, "disorganized and disconnected."

"Did you ever wonder why?"

"Why what?"

"Why it's such a struggle to get your arms around your info?"

Harold paused. "I guess I've never really developed a consistent way of organizing things. I just stick emails into folders and make up folder titles as I go along. Other times I just let emails pile up in my inbox. We're so busy these days, going from project to project with little administrative help. There's no time to get organized." He paused and then shot me a worried glance, "Why do *you* think I'm struggling?"

"I find that most professionals focus on *what* they store rather than *how* it's stored. They end up managing a heap of difficult-to-locate email and documents. That's inefficient..."

"...and stressful too," added Harold emphatically.

I nodded. "A lot of people that we speak to agree: Organizing 8,000 of anything without guidance and a solid plan doesn't make much sense, does it?"

Harold shook his head. "I should have taken the time to figure out a better system."

"I think you've done the best you could. Almost every client I work with starts from the same place."

"Well it's time for a change," said Harold, "So what's the plan, Coach?"

I smiled. "Today, you'll discover the most revolutionary aspect of the Hamster Revolution: a powerful new way to organize your folders called COTA.® If you like it, we'll begin setting up COTA on your computer. But first, I'd like to share three challenges with your current organizational system. I'll also provide ways that you can address these challenges. Whether or not you adopt COTA, these insights can help you design a better way to store your info. Sound good?"

"Sure," replied Harold, "Hey Coach, is COTA software?"

"No. It's an easy-to-use folder system. We start with four *primary folders* and then provide you with six storage secrets that make storing and retrieving information easier and more effective."

"What do you mean by *primary folders?*" asked Harold.

"When you go to the place in your computer where you store your documents or email, you'll see an initial list of storage folders that you've created, right? Those are your *primary* folders. Folders placed inside those folders are *sub-folders*. Okay?"

"Got it," said Harold, "So what's wrong with my current system?"

Challenge 1: Overlapping Categories

"First of all, you're using a number of *overlapping* primary folder categories. Have you ever looked for a document on your computer and had to hunt from one folder to the next thinking that it could be here or here or there?"

"All the time!" chuckled Harold. "It's frustrating."

"I know. Let me show you why that happens." I got up and began to write on Harold's whiteboard, "Here are the names of three of your actual email storage folders. I've also included the general categorization method that you use for each one."

Email Folder Name	Categorization Method
Spreadsheets	Filed by Type of Software
Stuff Sent by Boss	Filed by Sender
Training Programs	Filed by Content

"What's wrong with those folders?" asked Harold defensively. "I learned some of these in my time-management class."

"Individually, these are good folders. But taken together, they overlap and cause confusion. What if your **boss sends** you a **spreadsheet** related to a **training program**? Where do you file that message?"

Harold was about to say something but then he paused and frowned, "Okay, I see — that message could be stored in any one of these three folders. So when I come back to find it, I'll never know exactly where it is."

"And that *uncertainty*, caused by overlap, is the main reason why things are always 'vaporizing' on you. You've created a folder system where overlap is *the rule* rather than the exception. Over time, the *more* you use your folder system, the *harder* it is to find information. As you accumulate more and more stored documents with multiple hiding places, your system falls apart and suddenly you're lost in a vast wasteland of information."

"The harder I work, the harder I have to work," sighed Harold, appearing to sense the connection to his email woes. He was looking at his computer files as if seeing them for the first time. "And info-glut wins again."

"The key is to pick one method for categorizing your information and stick with it. Selecting a single method greatly reduces overlap, decreases uncertainty, and defeats info glut. We'll look at a great way to do that in just a moment."

"Okay, what else is wrong with my system?" asked Harold eagerly.

Challenge 2: Too Many Primary Folders

"You've created 57 primary email storage folders."

"So?"

"Each time you try to file or find an email, you have to decide between 57 possible email folders. What do you think about that?"

"57 choices, changing all the time," mused Harold. "That does sound a bit complicated."

"A bit?" I asked. "Try *a lot* complicated. If you owned a restaurant, would you list your food in a long alphabetical list of 57 items? No, you'd chunk your menus into three master categories: Breakfast, Lunch, and Dinner. Right?"

"Yes," agreed Harold.

"Now why would you do it that way?"

"So people could easily find what they wanted to order. I get it; it's kind of like the Dewey Decimal System in libraries or the Dairy section in a grocery store."

"Right," I said, "Our brains aren't good at juggling 57 options at one time.[13] It causes stress and fatigue. Unlike your filing system, effective storage systems break items down into logical chunks."

Harold twitched his whiskers thoughtfully as he stared at his computer files. "To find and file information fast, you're saying that I need to reduce the number of primary folders I use."

"Exactly, and that's why it's important to choose five to seven mutually exclusive primary folders that remain consistent over time. Again, you'll learn an easy way to do that in just a moment. But first, let's explore one final issue."

Challenge 3: Mismatched Folder Systems

"Because you create your folders on the fly, over time, all of your different storage areas have evolved *differently*. Your primary email folders are set up differently from your document folders." I pointed at the Blue Monster. "Your filing cabinet contains different folders than your computer folders. That's a problem because..."

"Nothing matches," interrupted Harold staring blankly at his computer screen. He surfed from his email folders over to his document folders. He looked at all the links he had stored in *My Favorites* and glanced over at his filing cabinet. "Everywhere I turn, I see different looking storage systems and I have to shift mental gears to remember how each one works."

"And that makes *multitasking* harder because you're constantly jumping between all of these mismatched storage systems all day long. That's why most people complain about their team's shared drive; it's another place they have to go that doesn't match."

"I despise our team's shared drive. Talk about a black hole..."

I let Harold vent a bit and then continued, "So the final key is to develop one simple folder system and extend it to *all* of the places where you store information. Now let me show you how COTA addresses everything we just discussed."

"Hold it." Harold raised his paw. "I want to learn about COTA, but what about desktop search software? Wouldn't that solve the problems you just mentioned?"

I got up and walked to the window. Turning to Harold, I said, "I like desktop search. But in my opinion, search is only half of the solution. I believe that it's much more important, from a workflow perspective, to actually *know* where your information is located. When you create an effective folder system, navigating to the right information suddenly becomes a breeze. Your information is ordered and accessible at all times. You can zoom in and grab what you need without having to think up keywords that may yield no hits or 1,000 hits. That's why I use desktop search as a complement to my COTA system."

"I guess I was hoping for a silver bullet," mused Harold.

"That's understandable," I said, "Millions of people can't find half of their emails and search can be very helpful. But a well-designed folder system helps you browse for ideas, best practices, and files that you'd never think to search for. It helps you see relationships between seemingly unrelated pieces of information in the electronic *and* hard copy worlds. For me, it's the difference between efficiently *managing knowledge* and endlessly *searching* for things. There's a big difference between knowing and searching. And Harold, we search only for things that are lost to us. But what if your information wasn't *lost* in the first place?"

Harold leaned forward, "Well, *lost* is exactly how I feel when I'm trying to find things these days. I want to learn COTA. I want to be in control of my information, instead of the other way around."

"Then let's go to COTA," I said walking from the window back to my chair.

11

STRATEGY 4: FILE AND FIND IT FAST WITH COTA

"I've helped lots of people organize their email and documents so that they could file and find everything fast. After working with hundreds of people with all different kinds of jobs in all different size companies I began to notice an intriguing pattern."

"What kind of pattern?" asked Harold.

"I started to notice that we were winding up with the same four primary business folders over and over again."

"But what four folders could possibly work for people from 50 different professions?" exclaimed Harold, looking a little nervous. "There can't be a one-size-fits-all solution."

"That's what I thought at first," I said. "It went against the grain of everything I'd been taught about storing information. So I kept trying to ignore the pattern, but it kept repeating."

"What did your clients think?" asked Harold. "Did the system work for them?"

"They were thrilled because the system was easy to use and didn't fall apart over time. At last they felt organized and in control. The quality of their work improved and their careers took off because the new system didn't require a lot of thought or memorization. And because the system was *universal*, they could use it even when they changed jobs."

"Useful," said Harold leaning forward, "No more reinventing the wheel whenever the wind changes direction."

I nodded. "Over the years, I continued to make improvements. I tried each idea on myself first to see if it really worked."

Harold furrowed his brow. "So you eat your own dog food?"

"Excuse me?"

"It's an expression. If you manufacture dog food, someone on your team has to taste it before feeding it to the dogs. Otherwise, how would you know if it really tastes good?"

I laughed. "I get it. And yes, I use COTA. It's on my computer, it's in my filing cabinet, and it's even on my team's shared document area. I eat my own dog food every day and I love it!"

"Good," said Harold looking relieved, "'cause I don't want to be a guinea pig!"

"Understood," I said with a smile.

"So what exactly is COTA?" asked Harold.

"COTA is an acronym for four primary folders that hold all of your business information. Once I describe the system, you'll see how it effectively organizes information while eliminating overlap."

I handed Harold another tent card. "Here's your fourth and final Hamster Revolution Tool. As you can see, I've placed all four

Hamster Revolution Tools onto one simple 4" x 6" card. You can place it by your computer as a constant reminder of everything you've learned."

Harold examined the tool carefully, "Wow, this is handy. But, I'm going to need a little help understanding COTA."

The COTA Tool	
COTA Folder	**Contains Business Info Relating to:**
1. **C**lients	Your team's internal or external clients
2. **O**utput	Your team's products and services
3. **T**eams	Your team
4. **A**dmin	Your non–core–job responsibilities

"Learning COTA is a little more involved than everything we've covered so far. So let's do a little exercise that will make it easier for you to understand its power and usefulness. Close your eyes for a second and take a deep breath."

Harold seemed reluctant, but when he saw that I was serious about the exercise, he closed his eyes and took a deep breath. "Okay, Okay. Let the COTA hypnosis begin," he grinned.

"Let's start with the COTA Team folder." I said, "Think back on all of the jobs you've had in the last 10 years."

"Okay," said Harold.

"Have you *ever* had a job where you weren't on some kind of team?"

Harold pondered this simple question, "No. Even when I sold advertising for my college newspaper, I was on a team."

"And so naturally, you had to store information *about* the team that you were on: things such as rosters, business plans, meeting notes, team projects?"

"Of course," smiled Harold with his eyes still closed. "OK, I think I get your point. Because being on a team is a *constant* in the business world, *Teams* is a useful primary folder for storing all information relating to teams."

"Right," I said. "This is the beginning of that pattern I was talking about a moment ago. Let's talk about the *Output* folder now. Were you ever on a business team that *didn't* produce or deliver a product, service, or process of some kind?

"Never," said Harold firmly, "A business team has to produce something of value. If it doesn't, it won't be around for long."

"Can you give me some examples of the *Output* produced by your current or past teams?" I asked.

"I worked in information technology for awhile and my team's *Output* was customer service for all of our company's computer users. When I worked in advertising sales for my college newspaper, we provided advertising space for local companies. In HR, we *Output* things such as Training Programs, the Benefits Program, and Productivity Programs."

"And you store a lot of information relating to the HR services you just described?"

Harold nodded, "Tons of information."

"So *Output* is also a useful primary folder for storing information, another *constant* as you called it. And if every job you've held has involved a *Team* that delivered *Output* wasn't there always some group of people on the *receiving* end of your *Team's Output*? HR doesn't push its training programs into outer space, does it?"

Harold still had his eyes closed. He seemed very relaxed, "Right. *Outputting* something to no one is futile. In HR, we *Output* our services to the other divisions such as Sales, Finance, and R&D. They're our internal *Clients*."

Harold was silent for a moment. Suddenly he opened his eyes, "Whoa. If *Teams* and *Output* are constants, then *Clients* must also be a constant. *Teams Output* value to *Clients*. That's what business is. That's why COTA worked for all of your clients despite the fact that they were in different industries. It's based on the process of business, which is universal and constant."

Harold eyed the four folders on the COTA tool: *Clients, Output, Teams,* and *Admin*. "I'm starting to get this."

"Do I need to convince you that you also store a great deal of *Admin* info?"

"No," laughed Harold. "*Admin* is inescapable! Your primary COTA folders actually make a lot of sense." He paused and frowned, "but does implementing them really make a huge difference?"

I smiled. "Remember the three challenges we just discussed? COTA has one categorization method: *content*. This eliminates the uncertainty that has caused so much confusion for you. And because COTA uses only four folders, it's easier to zoom to the information you need. You only need to know if you're searching for *Client, Output, Team,* or *Admin* info to start the location process. That's a lot easier than choosing between 57 options."

"Can I use COTA for all the different places I store information?" asked Harold.

"Every single one," I said. "COTA will eliminate the mental friction of multitasking. Whether you're searching for a key email or hard copy document, you have to remember only one simple organizational system: COTA."

"But how long will it take to set up COTA?" asked Harold cautiously.

"About one day."

"I don't know," protested Harold, "I'm awfully busy."

"So far, we both agree that the Hamster Revolution will save you 15 days a year. I'd like you to take one of those days and invest it into setting up COTA. Most COTA users make back their setup time within a couple weeks because suddenly, they can file and find their information in a flash."

"Sounds like a pretty good investment," admitted Harold.

"Do you want to get started?" I asked eagerly.

"One last question," said Harold, pointing at the whiteboard. "Why do you use numbers in front of the COTA folders?"

"When I set up the folders on my clients' computers, the *Admin* folder always came first because computers default to alphabetical order. That seemed wrong to me. I realized that by putting numbers in folder titles we could create a *consistent order* that more closely matches our universal *business priorities*. Over time, I found that it was much easier to work in an environment that reflected my values. So, I placed *Clients* at the top of the COTA order so that I would always be reminded to focus on my client needs. We placed *Admin* in the fourth slot because it's important, but not our top priority."

"Makes sense," said Harold looking nervously at his computer. "So what do we do first?"

Learning COTA: 1. Clients

"Let's start in *My Documents* by creating a new primary folder called *1. Clients*."

"Okay," said Harold as he created the *1. Clients* document folder. He smiled as it moved to the top of his folder list. Harold realized that he had already created folders for most of his internal clients, such as IT and Sales. He simply clicked and dragged the pre-existing folders into the *Clients* folder. We reworked a few things in each folder and deleted a number of outdated documents. In the end, Harold's *Clients* folder looked like this:

1. **Clients**
   - Finance
   - IT Dept.
   - Marketing
   - R&D
   - Sales

"Now you've got all of your client information in one neat place. We'll talk about shaping the middle layers of COTA in a moment. But for now, let's get the four primary COTA folders installed on your computer."

Learning COTA: 2. Output

"Great," said Harold. "I'll bet you want me to create the *2. Output* folder now, right?"

"Right. And these are the products or services your team delivers."

Harold's eyes brightened. "HR *Outputs* a menu of services to our internal clients including Benefits, Recruiting, Productivity Programs, and Training and Development. I have folders for most of those services already."

Harold clicked and dragged a bunch of folders into his *Output* section. He created a couple others and then stopped and frowned, "Here's a problem. This folder is a special productivity project that I did for R&D alone. It could go in either *Output* as a productivity project or *Clients* —R&D. I thought you said that COTA *eliminated* overlap?"

"It does," I said. "We've created a simple rule for this situation. What you've just described is a kind of a tie between two possible COTA storage locations. When you're in this situation, simply use the actual *order of the COTA folders* to break the tie. So a folder that could fit into both *Clients* and *Output* would always go under *Clients* because it comes first in the COTA order."

Harold was thoughtful, "Hey that's actually a good idea because when I'm confronted with another tie and you're not around to coach me, I'll just look at COTA and boom, I'll have my answer."

"Here's another simple COTA rule," I added. "Let's say you're a widget salesperson and you receive a price list containing prices for all 12 kinds of widgets that you sell. Instead of creating a new folder every time you need to store something like this, I would recommend that you use *The General*."

"What general?" asked Harold.

By creating a *General Output* folder, you're strategically creating a place for information that relates to multiple *Output* items. This strategy is also useful if you have a lot of clients."

"So creating *General Clients* and *General Output* folders makes sense because at some point in time, I'll receive information that pertains to all of my clients or all of my output services?" asked Harold.

I nodded. "So the only two COTA rules are: (1) Use the COTA hierarchy to break ties and (2) Use *The General* for documents that pertain to multiple items within a COTA category."

Now Harold's *Output* section looked like this:

2. Output
- Benefits
- General Output
- Productivity Programs
  - Accountability Project
- Recruiting
- Training/Development

"The next COTA category is Teams… right, Coach?"

Learning COTA: 3. Teams

"How many business teams are you on, Harold?" I asked.

"I'm on the Global HR Team and the Organizational Effectiveness Team," replied Harold. As we scanned his folder list, Harold had pre-existing folders for these teams. He created a *3. Teams* primary folder and dragged the pre-existing folders into it. He realized that a number of other sub-folders fit neatly into this section, so he clicked and dragged them as well. His *Teams* section now looked like this:

3. Teams
- Global HR Team
- Org. Effectiveness Team

"And *Admin* is the final primary COTA Folder?" asked Harold, with a growing sense of excitement.

Learning COTA: 4. Admin

I nodded and pointed to the whiteboard. "As we've discussed, *Admin* consists of *non–core–job* tasks… things like your individual compensation information, your…"

Harold rolled his eyes. "This one's easy. Everyone's got *Admin*. Its stuff like expense reports, my computer information, travel information, attendance reports, right?

"Exactly. *Admin* is also your overflow category for that rare file that doesn't fit into the primary COTA folders."

Harold made a *4. Admin* folder and dragged a bunch of his current folders into the COTA structure. Here is what his final *Admin* section looked like:

4. Admin
- Achievement Folder
- Artwork
- Attendance Reports
- Benefits (individual)
- Business Wisdom
- Expense Report
- Forms
- IT and Communications Info
- Policies and Procedures
- Travel
- Vendor Info & Receipts

Harold spent some time surfing through his new COTA folders. He tweaked some titles and created some sub-folders. He still had about 10 remaining folders that didn't seem to fit into the COTA system. Most of them were overlap folders including the *Sent by Boss* folder, the *Urgent* folder, and the *Spreadsheet* folder. Harold took some time and sorted through these folders. He realized that a lot of the content could be deleted or easily transferred into a particular COTA folder.

Harold's COTA folder system now looked like this:

1. Clients
- Finance
- General Clients
- IT Dept.
- Marketing
- R&D
  - R&D Productivity Project
- Sales

2. Output
- Benefits
- General Output
- Productivity Programs
  - Accountability Project
- Recruiting
- Training/Development

3. Teams
- Global HR Team
- Org. Effectiveness Team

4. Admin
- Achievement Folder
- Artwork
- Attendance Reports
- Business Wisdom
- IT & Communications
- Expense Report
- Forms
- Training
- Travel
- Vendor Info & Receipts

"It seems so neat and ordered," said Harold. "So clean."

"Our time is running out, Harold, so I want to give you an important gift." I handed Harold a sheet of paper. "These are the Six Secrets of COTA. Each secret increases the speed and power of the COTA system. Most of the secrets will even help non-COTA users to store information more efficiently. Your homework assignment is to review and implement these Six Secrets over the next week. They're easy to use and you'll be amazed at how they streamline your workflow. If you get stuck, give me a call or visit hamsterrevolution.com for help."

The Six Secrets of COTA*

1. **Use the *Details View* in *My Documents*.** Within *My Documents*, *Details View* allows you to see all documents and folders in a neat vertical layout. It also uses smaller folder icons that make it easier to scan down and find the file you need. Set all Windows *My Documents* folders to *Details View* by going to *My Documents* and selecting *Tools/Folder Options/View/Apply to All Folders*.

2. **Prioritize with numbers.** When confronted by a long list of folders or documents, streamline workflow by adding a number to the title of four or five of the most often used items to bring them to the top of the list.

3. **Use Power Drafts for consistency.** A *Power Draft* is a master folder containing frequently used sub-folders. Copy and rename the *Power Draft* whenever a new folder is needed. For example, you have 20 *Client* folders and sub-folders that all have different names. Unify them over time by creating a standard *Client Folder Power Draft* and copying it whenever you get a new client.

4. **Save time by maximizing access.** Windows users: Maximize access to your information by creating desktop shortcuts to *all four* COTA My Documents folders. Then drag the four shortcuts to your lower horizontal toolbar. (You may have to right-click and unlock the lower toolbar.) This gives you lightning fast access to COTA documents even when you have many other documents open. You can also load the *My Documents* COTA folders into *My Favorites*. Once loaded, you will discover an amazingly fast tool that allows you to zoom in and out of COTA folders without having to open new windows.

5. **Create COTA folders for Net Links.** Many users have hundreds of Internet links but have never created a folder system for them. Create COTA folders for your links in *My Favorites* and you'll be able to manage twice as many links twice as fast.

6. **Convert your filing cabinet to COTA.** Take all of your folders out of your hard-copy filing cabinet and sort them into COTA categories. If possible, use consistent markers, folders, folder-holders, etc. to create a less chaotic view. Try to match the system on your computer as closely as possible and make sure your filing cabinet is within arm's reach of your desk.

Harold read through the list to see if he understood each secret, "Most of these make sense. But I'd like to learn more about *Power Drafts.*"

I nodded. "You have multiple *Client* folders in your primary COTA *Clients* folder, right?"

"Sure," said Harold looking at his internal clients, which included Sales, R&D, and Finance.

"We've discovered that multiple *Client, Output,* or *Team* folders often contain the same kinds of information. But because you create them on the fly, all of the folders look different, which slows navigation in the middle layer of COTA."

Harold looked thoughtful. "I know what you mean. I have projects and proposals for all of my clients, but I've named them in many different ways."

"The solution is to create what we call a *Power Draft.* A Power Draft is simply a master folder template with four or five standard sub-folders in a standard order. When you join a new team or take on a new client, you can copy the Power Draft and rename it." I walked to the whiteboard, "Your *Client Power Draft* folder could look like this:

- **ZZ Client Power Draft**
  1. Account Info
  2. Proposals
  3. Projects
  4. PO's
  5. Invoices

"And that way," reasoned Harold, "All my *Client* and *Team* folders would be organized in a consistent way."

"You've got it," I replied, "It's much easier to navigate in familiar surroundings. I usually put a ZZ in front of the title of my Power Drafts so that they slip to bottom of the folder list. That way, I know where to find them."

Harold was getting excited, "Hey! Power Drafting could be really useful for all of the training programs I develop for Foster and Schrubb. Every program has an invitation, a presentation, a workbook. We could create a Power Draft for our team's shared drive. Right now, every training folder looks different. What a mess."

"Your life is getting easier by the minute," I laughed.

As our time drew to a close, Harold showed me a couple of email folders containing several hundred messages that would be very time-consuming to transfer over to COTA. I told him not to worry about transferring all the information. Instead, he could use the folders *as is* for a few months and transfer information over to COTA whenever he encountered something valuable. I told Harold that in my experience, most users find that they can back up and then delete these large email folders after three or four months. In that time, most of the important emails have been opened and saved into COTA during the normal course of business.

"Any final words of wisdom, Coach?" asked Harold as he walked me to the elevator.

"No, but I've got a question for you. What's motivating you to adopt COTA?"

"It seems like my choice is COTA or chaos. I'm sick of chaos. I'll try to implement the Six COTA Secrets this week. I'll also keep using the 1-2-3 and A-B-C Email Tools."

"Fantastic. Where would you like to hold our final wrap-up meeting?"

"How about the same time next week at the Blue Sky Café?" suggested Harold.

"Sounds great," I said as I shook Harold's paw. "See you next week!"

12

A BLUE SKY WRAP UP

Harold and I sat on tall stools at a small table in the Blue Sky Café. This was our final Hamster Revolution meeting and we were toasting Harold's excellent progress. Harold took a celebratory swig from his cup of espresso. Although the cup was small, it seemed rather large in his little paws. The staff, who knew Harold as a regular, seemed nonplussed to be serving coffee to a hamster. But many of the customers stared in disbelief. It was easy to ignore their gawking: After all, we had important things to discuss.

"It's been an amazing week," said Harold. "I converted everything to COTA and I've never been more organized. You were right about email and filing being interrelated."

"How does it feel?" I asked.

Harold paused, "Calm and focused. That's how I feel. On the email side, I'm sending and receiving clear, concise, and necessary messages. Just about everyone's agreed to use the 1-2-3 and A-B-C Email

Tools. And COTA has eliminated a lot of the uncertainty in my life. Now I can quickly find the documents I need to get things done. I'm still learning and I still have some fine-tuning to do, but I finally have a plan that simplifies the management of all my information. It's a huge step forward for me."

"And what about your goals?" I asked.

"Kyle and I found a great karate place and I'm putting together my initial plan for the Accountability project."

Feeling satisfied that Harold was on his way to reclaiming his life, I asked him if he had any final questions or comments.

Harold looked excited. "Coach, I've found some different ways to use COTA."

"You did?" I asked with a smile.

"Yes, I was jotting down my priorities for this week and I spontaneously began sorting my tasks into COTA categories. I was thinking things such as, *Hey, this is an Admin thing that can wait 'til tomorrow but preparing for this Client meeting is absolutely critical.*" COTA seems to make prioritizing easier. Then at yesterday's HR Team meeting we talked about how one of our internal clients wasn't very happy with a training program we delivered. And I found myself talking about how we needed to make sure our *Output* is always in line with what the *Client* needs. Every day I find that I'm using COTA for a lot of different things."

"That's because COTA mirrors the natural flow of business," I said, taking out a pen and sketching a little flowchart on a napkin. "Like we discussed: *Teams* Deliver *Output* to *Clients*. Good clients return value by paying, praising, or supporting your team. *Admin* is a natural by-product of this simple process. One key is that *Admin* shouldn't come between a *Team* and its *Clients*. This process will exist in every job you'll ever hold."

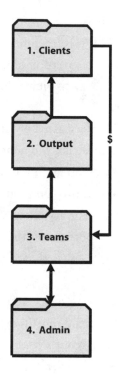

"So naturally, COTA has other uses," said Harold.

I nodded. "Any other COTA stories to share?" I asked. "I love hearing them."

"Yes. Janet, my administrative assistant, really likes COTA. I showed it to her and she agreed to give it a try. I was traveling one day last week and she was able to find several documents in my filing cabinet while I was gone."

"In the Blue Monster?" I asked.

"Now that it's organized by COTA, it has morphed back into a filing cabinet," laughed Harold. "The important thing was that Janet was able to find the right information to help an internal client with an urgent problem. In the past, she wouldn't even have tried."

"That's just the tip of the iceberg in terms of how your team can become more efficient with COTA. Remember, COTA is flexible. If some team members want to use a variation of COTA, that's Okay. But it is nice to have a common way to view information. Wait until you reorganize that shared drive."

"I can't wait," agreed Harold. He shifted on his stool and took another sip of his espresso. "Let me ask you another question," he said. "I have a couple teammates who are interested in COTA. But something is causing them to hold off. One colleague is a manager who considers his boss to be his primary client. Another is a manager who considers the people who report to her to be her clients. This made COTA kind of confusing because these folks regard members of their own teams as clients."

"I would simply explain that designating your team's *real world* clients as *Clients* within COTA is the most practical way to use COTA. This shouldn't diminish anyone's passion for providing excellent service to teammates. However, the COTA hierarchy is a helpful way to visualize your team's role in a broader context."

"That ties into my Accountability Project," said Harold. "Right now, we're seeing productivity decline along with internal client satisfaction levels. Some departments aren't helping others as much as they could. Eventually it trickles down to the service we give our real clients."

"It's a universal business challenge," I said.

"But like you just said, COTA keeps teams focused on their clients," Harold reasoned. "I see it in myself. Over the past week, I've begun to pay more attention to the *Output* that I'm delivering to my internal *Clients*."

"And, if everyone in HR adopts COTA, your entire team will be more client-focused," I suggested. "And as a result, your clients will return more value to your team. This can impact staffing needs, funding requests, and the overall vitality of your team, division, and entire organization."

We sat for a moment quietly sipping our coffee. Then I decided to change the topic. "Harold, what happens to an employee's information when they leave Foster and Schrubb?"

"We just scrub that information off the outgoing person's hard drive and give their computer to someone else. We try to have them download important things that the new person needs, but that rarely happens."

"So all that stored information and knowledge disappears?"

"Yup," sighed Harold.

"Ideas, plans, and projects go up in a puff of smoke. This may sound a bit dramatic, but it sounds like a significant portion of your company's knowledge sits on *death row*, waiting for someone to get promoted or retire."

"Or get fired," added Harold.

"And when they're gone, their stored knowledge dies."

"Unless they take it with them to a competitor," groaned Harold. "Then it doesn't die. It comes back to haunt us. We've already lost a lot of business that way."

"You have?"

Harold nodded. "And after someone leaves, the new person comes in and struggles for three or four months trying to find the information and perspective they need to get the job done."

Harold paused, deep in thought. Suddenly, he sat up straight.

"But if everyone knew COTA, it would be different. We could develop a process for transferring the information between outgoing and incoming colleagues. People would be able to see who their clients really are. They would have a kind of contextual compass that would allow them to explore all that accumulated information more efficiently."

Harold was excited by his vision of a more efficient Foster and Schrubb, "Actually, wider adoption of all four Hamster Revolution strategies could have a huge impact on our bottom line," he said, seeing the possibilities.

I felt energized and excited for Harold. Our time was coming to a close and Harold seemed so different from when we first met. "You've done an amazing job, Harold. This is the beginning of an incredible journey for you. Could you sum up your experience over the last few weeks? What are the most important things you've learned?"

Harold thought for a moment and smiled. "When it comes to battling info-glut, I've learned that using the Hamster Revolution strategies is the best *investment* you can make. If you apply the tools and work hard, you can restore order and balance to your life. As far as spreading the revolution goes, start by coaching one teammate, get them excited, and then move on to the next one. If you can help an entire team start a conversation around email challenges, you're halfway home. Share your experiences and shortcomings and connect them to Hamster Revolution insights. Catch everyone emailing something right and a small grassroots movement will emerge."

I remained silent, hoping that Harold would continue. After a thoughtful pause, he said, "When it comes to being an Info-Coach, *walking the walk* is critical. You've got to eat your own dog food or people won't listen to a word you say. You have to leave your comfort zone but it's worth it. When people complain about email, turn their frustration into motivation by giving them effective tools and helping them see the big picture. Email really does add up."

I smiled at Harold's insight. He tilted his head back and thought some more. "Study info-glut," he said slowly. "Find out where it's slowing you down and take action. It's a resourceful enemy that stands between you and your lifetime goals. You can't unlock your fullest potential when you're drowning in email. You can't be a confident leader if you're constantly struggling to find things. These days, you have to have the right information at the right time if you want to win."

"And finally," said Harold as we settled our bill, "I've learned that you have to keep your eyes on the prize."

"What does that mean for you?" I asked as I took the last satisfying sip of my mochaccino, the sip that's got all the chocolate at the bottom.

"Right now it means spending that father-son time with Kyle, being there for him, helping him through this tough patch he's in." Harold's voice wavered and he took a deep breath, "And at work, it means completing the Accountability Project without falling behind. If I can do that, the revolution is a success and my life is back on track."

I was very impressed with Harold's summary. He had absorbed a great deal in a very short time. "You've made amazing progress, Harold," I said as we walked out onto a sunny city sidewalk.

"Coach," said Harold, turning to face me and extending his paw. "Thanks for all the insight, support, and encouragement."

"Good-bye, Harold," I said. "Remember, I'm here when you need me. I've really enjoyed working with you."

"And I, you."

Harold turned and strode confidently down the busy sidewalk. Pedestrians turned in amazement as he walked by. Harold didn't seem to notice. As he rounded the corner he glanced back and raised a fisted paw in the air. It was a sign of determination and purpose. I raised my fist in the air in a show of solidarity and just like that — Harold was gone.

EPILOGUE

"Hey!"

I looked up from my computer screen and was startled to see a stranger's head poking into my office.

"I was just passing by and I thought I'd say hello."

"I'm sorry," I said, "Do... do we know each other?"

"Know each other? Coach, you practically turned my whole life around!"

Then it hit me. "Harold?"

"Well, who else could it be? C'mon, Coach, it's only been six months since our last face-to-face meeting."

"Oh! Of course! Come on in, Harold."

Harold strode into my office and I was amazed to see the transformation. He was an energetic, 35-year-old man with intense brown eyes. He wore a dark blue business suit and carried a sharp looking black leather briefcase. And there was something else... he looked confident and relaxed. Harold looked me right in the eyes as we shook hands.

"I just wanted to stop by to thank you, Coach. Everything you taught me about email and COTA has made a huge difference in my life. Carol and I have never been happier."

"And Kyle?" I asked.

"Check this out," Harold flipped open his PDA and showed me a picture of Kyle and him at karate class, "We're both green belts!"

"And the Accountability Project?" I asked.

"Our leadership team put it on the fast track. It's been rolled out to everyone at Foster and Schrubb; 5,000 people have learned how to take ownership of their team's mission. Internal and external client service ratings are way up — profits, too. The execs are thrilled."

"Excellent," I said as I stood up.

My next meeting was about to start, so I walked Harold out to our lobby and wished him well. As the elevator door opened, we were surprised to see a flustered-looking female hamster step out. She was dressed in a sharp gray business suit and carrying a maroon briefcase.

"Excuse me," she said, as Harold stepped into the elevator.

"Can you tell me where I can find the Info-Coach?"

"I'm the Info-Coach," I said, extending my hand. "Pleased to meet you."

"I'm Iris and this is embarrassing to admit, but I've got a real problem with email. I need help!"

Harold and I exchanged a silent smile as the elevator door slowly closed.

"My job is to help professionals manage their email *before* it manages them, Iris."

"Well maybe I'm in the right place after all," she sighed as we walked down the hall toward my office.

"Say, Iris, do you like coffee?" I asked.

"I'm practically addicted," she replied.

Revolution was in the air.

APPENDIX 1:

FAST ANSWERS FOR BUSY HAMSTERS

Over the next few months, Harold called several times to ask questions. What follows is a summary of those brief conversations.

Harold: Are there any email technology tips I could use to be more productive?

Info-Coach: Absolutely. We've created a free Top Tech Tips Newsletter that you can subscribe to on hamsterrevolution.com.

Harold: Should I answer email on the fly or block out time?

Info-Coach: I recommend blocking out 30-minute periods in advance. You can process email more rapidly in *batches* because you can give it your undivided attention.

I also recommend disconnecting your ding — the sound or visual image your computer makes when an email arrives. Most of the time, you don't need to be notified every time an email comes in. If you keep your ding on, it's like planning 40–50 interruptions into every business day. On average, it takes over a minute to regain refocus after being distracted by an incoming email.[14] These distractions sap your energy and slow you down. Another way to limit email interruption is to set your email to synchronize every 30 minutes instead of every 2 or 3 minutes. We show you how on hamsterrevolution.com.

Harold: I ran into several people with email inboxes containing over a thousand emails. Any advice for these folks?"

Info-Coach: Because critical actions and information can be buried in an inbox jammed with thousands of emails, I recommend blocking off a half day and sorting the inbox in a number of different ways to rapidly reduce the number. First, *Sort by date* and delete as many outdated and irrelevant emails as possible. Next, *Sort by sender*. In many cases, you'll often find that a particular sender's email has lost relevance to what you're doing and can all be deleted at once. Next, *Sort by subject* and look for email categories such as *Action, Request, Delivery,* or *Confirmation* emails. These signify important emails that may need to be saved or reviewed before deletion.

Finally, you can sort your inbox by document size. This will bring up emails with large and potentially important attachments. After three hours you'll find that you have significantly reduced the number of emails in your inbox. Make sure you keep track of the opportunities you unearth as you address your backlog. You'll be amazed at the gems that are buried at the bottom of your email inbox ocean. You may need to repeat the process, but it's worth your time and attention. After deleting useless information, spend time aggressively saving important emails and attachments with clear future value.

Harold: Is Hamster Revolution team training available?

Info-Coach: Yes. You can learn about live and virtual Hamster Revolution training at hamsterrevolution.com.

Harold: Should I strive to have zero messages in my inbox?

Info-Coach: No, but I do recommend choosing a concrete goal for the optimal number of emails you would like to have in your inbox at any one time. Like it or not, we all use our inbox as a secondary task list. If you have 30 or 40 emails in your inbox, you can actually glance through them pretty quickly and see what needs to be done. I arbitrarily chose 42 as my target number.

Harold: Any tips for deleting or storing incoming email?

Info-Coach: My motto is *Store Less — Find More*. Aggressively delete any message that has limited *future value*. If you can't see a clear purpose for the email, ditch it. Also, if the content of a particular email can be easily found by searching online, on the intranet, or rapidly delivered from another source, such as a co-worker, you don't need to save it.

Harold: Can you show me how COTA might work for some different professions?

Info-Coach: Here's a grid that gives a general idea of how COTA works for different jobs.

COTA Category				
Job Type	**1. Clients**	**2. Output**	**3. Teams**	**4. Admin**
Sales	External customers who buy or influence what you sell	Actual products, services, and value-added items sold or offered to clients	Teams to which you belong. For example, District Sales Team, Regional Sales Team, Networking Associations, etc.	Benefits Company car Travel Finances Forms Corporate PR Expense Report
HR	Internal customers including IT, Sales, R&D, etc.	Hiring services Benefits package Payroll, etc. Associations	HR team and sub-teams Cross-functional teams Learning and dev. Compliance	All of the above
Doctor	Patients and other institutions that directly control access to patients. For example, hospitals or HMOs.	Healthcare info and other kinds of services related to the health of patients. For example, how to set a broken bone	Office team Associations Hospital Committee Local Medical Group	All of the above
IT	Internal customers including HR, Sales, R&D, etc.	Information related to the IT services and equipment you provide.	IT team and sub-teams Cross-functional teams Associations	All of the above
R&D	Potential consumers	Company's products and value-added products Research data Product development data	R&D team and sub-teams Associations	All of the above

Harold: COTA is for business info. What about my personal info?
Info-Coach: Inevitably, you will store some personal information on your business computer. For now, I would recommend creating a fifth primary folder and labeling it *5. Personal.* We've also created a powerful system for managing personal information called PAO. You can learn more about PAO on hamsterrevolution.com.

Harold: I store half of my info in email folders and the other in My Documents. Isn't it confusing to store things in two places?

Info-Coach: It is. I prefer to store as much as possible in My Documents. Compared to email folder systems, My Documents is much more powerful and simple to use. I find it easier to create, copy, view, and move things in My Documents. Another benefit is that anytime you need to save, insert, browse, or open a document, Windows defaults to the My Documents view and boom... there are my COTA folders and documents. This really pays off when I am inserting things into emails.

Here's a neat trick: from within any Microsoft document, simply hit the f12 key. This allows you to save directly to your COTA system within My Documents. This works for Word, Excel, PowerPoint, and even Outlook emails. If you save both emails and documents into a single powerful document management system, you've got one-stop shopping for all your info. Two words of caution: First, many organizations need to keep email in email folders for legal or security reasons. Be sure to get approval from your IT folks before saving email into My Documents. If they say, "no", you can always use COTA within your email folders. Finally, we just don't know how technology will change down the road so it's impossible to guarantee that email saved into My Documents will be always be recoverable.

APPENDIX 2:

CASE STUDY: CAPITAL ONE'S EMAIL EFFICIENCY SOLUTION

This case study underscores the value of implementing Hamster Revolution insights across a large organization. This case study can also be found at hamstserrevolution.com.

A. SUMMARY

Challenge: Capital One is an organization that constantly strives to maximize productivity. When internal surveys revealed that email overload was a growing productivity challenge, Capital One's Productivity Team took action.

Solution: The Capital One Productivity Team partnered with Mike Song and Tim Burress from Cohesive Knowledge Solutions, Inc. (CKS) to develop a groundbreaking email efficiency workshop. The Capital One Productivity Team played a major role in shaping the program. The workshop contained insights and exercises found in

The Hamster Revolution and other CKS seminars. Over 2,000 Capital One associates participated in this extremely successful learning and development experience.

B. SITUATION

Capital One (COF) has earned a sterling reputation for innovation, customer service, and leadership in the diversified financial services sector. Capital One manages $103 billion in assets for over 50 million customers worldwide.

In response to internal surveys, Capital One's Productivity Team isolated email as a major opportunity to increase productivity. Associates reported that email was consuming more than 30% of their work day. Internal surveys reflected growing concerns relating to the quality and quantity of email.

C. APPROACH

Capital One's Productivity Team, led by Matt Koch, Director of Productivity and Knowledge Management, made the bold decision to design an email productivity training solution with the following principles in mind:

- **Grounded by data:** Partnering with CKS, Capital One gathered as much information as possible via focus groups, surveys, external research, etc.
- **Customize and target solution:** The workshop objectives were carefully tailored to reflect the exact needs of Capital One associates. Capital One survey data was incorporated into the workshop to gain added buy-in from participants.
- **Fit the solution to the culture:** Capital One has a corporate culture that expects excellence while always doing the right thing by the customer, the associate, and the company. The workshop was designed to resonate with these core values.

- **Apply intellectual rigor:** Actual results were measured carefully against workshop goals and a pre-intervention baseline survey to validate participants' 75-minute time investment in the email productivity workshop. 2000 surveys containing over 100,000 individual question responses were collected and analyzed.

D. WORKSHOP CONTENT

The powerful email efficiency workshop developed by Capital One and CKS contained a series of engaging exercises, best practices, and tools that helped participants improve the overall value of email. Some of the elements of the program included:

- Discussion of email challenges
- Review of survey data
- The 1-2-3 and A-B-C Email Productivity Tools
- Exercises that contrasted good and poor emails
- Calculation exercises
- Role plays that helped participants gain Info-Coaching experience
- Written commitments to change behavior

In most cases, participants attended with their teams. This created a lively environment in which team members could discuss ongoing email concerns while creating powerful new team email strategies. Many coaching conversations took place during the seminars. Associates learned:

- How to send fewer email messages
- How to create clear, concise, and actionable email
- How to coach others to become more proficient at email

E. RESULTS

Two months after training, a follow-up survey revealed that:

- **Email decreased by 21%.** Associates reported a 21% reduction in total email sent. There was also a 10% reduction in email received, which demonstrates that the *Send Less — Get Less* concept works in the real world. Participants also reported a 23% drop in the time they spent processing email.

- **Email quality improved by 51%.** Associates reported an impressive 51% increase in email quality over baseline. Clear, concise, and actionable email naturally helps associates accomplish more in less time.

- **11.3 days saved.** Associates reported that they were on track to save 11.3 days per year on average. This figure did not take into account dramatic improvements in email quality, which are likely to have further decreased email processing time.

- **Leadership gains.** The workshop helped to empower associates to take control of the email environment via Info-Coaching. 60 days after training, the percentage of associates comfortable with email coaching rose from 47% to 75%.

- **One year post-training survey metrics.** Capital One and CKS conducted a One-Year Post Training Survey to determine if results could be sustained over time. The findings were extremely positive:

  - 88% continued to leverage workshop best practices.
  - 83% would recommend the workshop to *all* associates.
  - 80% believed that the workshop made them more productive.
  - 77% indicated that they continued to apply coaching principles gained in the workshop.

F. CONCLUSION

The Capital One Productivity Team did an excellent job of diagnosing and addressing a growing productivity challenge: email overload. They partnered with Cohesive Knowledge Solutions *www.cohesiveknowledge.com* to develop a highly effective, breakthrough learning experience that resulted in major time savings, improved productivity, and a better work/life balance for associates. Results were sustained over one full year.

Notes

1 Song, Michael and Burress, Tim "Info-Glut and the K-Worker," CKS White Paper, 2005.

2 Feldman, Susan "The High Cost of Not Finding Information," *KM World*, vol. 13, issue 3, 2004, available at www.KMWorld.com.

3 Hallerman, David, "2004 Email Marketing Report," eMarketer.com, 2004.

4 Song, Michael and Burress, Tim "Info-Glut and the K-Worker," CKS White Paper, 2005.

5 Cavanagh, Christina *Managing Your E-mail: Thinking Outside the Inbox*, John Wiley and Sons, 2003, p. 159.

6 Song, Michael and Burress, Tim "Info-Glut and the K-Worker," CKS White Paper, 2005.

7 Song, Michael and Burress, Tim "Info-Glut and the K-Worker," CKS White Paper, 2005.

8 Leland, Karen, and Bailey, Keith *Customer Service for Dummies*, IDG Books, 1999, excerpted from "Like it or Not, Voice-Mail Is Here to Stay," Sterling Consulting Group, 2004 Press Release.

9 Song, Michael and Burress, Tim "Info-Glut and the K-Worker," CKS White Paper, 2005.

10 Hallerman, David "2004 Email Marketing Report," eMarketer.com, 2004.

11 Song, Michael and Burress, Tim "Info-Glut and the K-Worker," CKS White Paper, 2005.

12 Feldman, Susan "The High Cost of Not Finding Information," *KM World*, vol. 13, issue 3, 2004, available at www.KMWorld.com.

13 Miller, George "The Magical Number Seven," *The Psychological Review,* vol. 63, 1956, pp. 81–97.

14 Jackson, Thomas Dawson, Ray and Wilson, Darren (Danwood Group/Loughborough University), "Evaluating the Effect of Email Interruptions within the Workplace," presented at EASE Conference (Evaluation and Assessment in Software Engineering), Keele University, 2002.

Acknowledgements

The authors would like to acknowledge and praise the incredible contributions of all the brilliant people who helped create this book:

Matt Koch of the Capital One Productivity Team: Your leadership and insight have been invaluable. Thanks for giving us the privilege of collaborating with you and 2,000 Capital One Associates on a groundbreaking knowledge management project.

Elena Song: Thanks for giving us your time and talent, even though you had screenwriting deadlines for Disney, DreamWorks, and Paramount. Your amazing editing, nonstop creative ideas, and ability to keep a straight face while discussing business hamsters helped bring Harold to life.

Bill Kirwin from Gartner: Thanks for being a trusted friend and long-time mentor. Your wisdom flows through everything we do.

Ken Blanchard and Marcus Buckingham: We've learned so much from you over the years. Thanks for lending your voices to The Hamster Revolution. We're deeply honored!

Steve Piersanti from BK publishing: Your brilliant advice reshaped our ideas and helped us create a more reader-centric book. Thanks for your honesty and insight.

Scott Blanchard, Madeleine Homan, Linda Miller, and James Flaherty; Thanks for being wise coaches who've taught us how to help people feel perfect as they act on their best intentions and step into their power.

Mark Forsyth, Margie Blanchard, and Debbie Blanchard from The Ken Blanchard Companies: Thanks for opening doors that we never could have opened ourselves. Your vision and support are greatly appreciated.

Steve Stone and the Infoflows Team: Thanks for building our understanding of software and technology. We can't thank you enough.

Ric Torres of Best Practices: Your business acumen is off the charts! Thanks for the excellent advice, practical ideas, and relentless support.

The authors would also like to thank these fabulous friends and family members who helped us realize a dream:

The entire Song, Halsey, and Burress families, Nicholas and Jake Halsey, Elaine, Jeff, Rox, Jordan and Kendra White, Mary Duncan, Martha Lawrence, Jeevan Sivasubramaniam, Mike Crowley, Pat Zigarmi, Kathy Cuff, Lisa Smedley, Kate Orf, Rubin Rodriguez, Dan Glaser, Nancy Jordan, Charlotte Jordan, Kevin Small, Richard Andrews, Christina Cavanaugh (author of the wonderful *Managing Your Email*), Tom and Nancy Patton, Pam Wiggins, Doug and Cindy Cole, Sean Dailey, Marilyn Kirwin, David Silver, Tom McKee, Steven Covey, Ellen Song, Al and Mary Song, Oreann "Mamaw" Miller, Vic Miller, Garrett Miller, Adam and Michelle Raiti, Doug and Marcia Fazzina, Tony Sheehan, Megan Kahn, Scott Schoenborn, Tim Reichert, Chris Ogle, Chris Dormer, Cory Brouer, Dave and Bridget O'Connor, Lisa Lelas, Patti Danos, Lisa Hiott, John Ireland, Nic Oatridge, Liz Kearns, Jeff and Allison Burress, and info-hamsters everywhere.

Index

Numbers
1-2-3 Email Quantity Tool, 20–21, 28
24-Hour Rule, 27
six secrets of COTA, 92

A
A-B-C Email Quality Tool, 41–42, 46–51
  action summary, 46–48
  background section, 48–49
    define and limit attachments, 49
    keep emails to execs concise, 49
    key points, 48
  close section, 49
    auto-signature, 5
    extensive niceties, 49
    next steps, 49
accept coaching, 55, 62
action content, 44

admin, 85, 89–90, 98
appropriate email, 24–27
  24 hour rule, 27
  angry email, 27, 67
  compliant, 24
  fact checking websites, 27
  inoffensive, 25
  joke email, 25–26
  professional, 25
  wise words of wisdom messages, (hoaxes), 26
Ask Before You Send questions, 20, 24

B
Blanchard, Ken, 11–12, 120–121, 126
Burress, Tim, 113, 121, 129

C
calculating email volume, 13

case study, Capital One, 113–117
  approach, 114–115
  challenge, 113
  results, 116
  situation, 114
  solution, 113
  workshop content, 115
copying recipients, (Cc), 30
Cc complaints, 30
clear email example, 8
Client Folder Power Draft, 92
clients, 84–87, 98
Cohesive Knowledge Solutions,
  (CKS), 126, 128
cohesiveknowledge.com,
  117, 126
confirmed content, 43
COTA®, locate information
  system, 75, 82
  admin, 85, 89–90, 98
  business priorities, 86
  clients, 84–87, 98
  COTA tool, 83–
  details view in My
    Documents, 92
  filing cabinet
    conversion, 93
  grid, 109–110
  hierarchy, 88
  maximize access, 93
  netlink folders, 93
  output, 84–85, 87–89, 98
    general clients folders, 88
    general output folders, 88
  Power Drafts for
    consistency, 92, 94
  prioritize with numbers, 92
  storage folders, 76
  teams, 84–85, 89, 98
  The General for
    documents, 88
COTA, explanation of, 109–111
COTA grid, 109
COTA to prioritize, 44, 86,
  92, 98

D

delivery content, 43
details view, 92
dig up the context, 47–48
distribution lists, 30

E

email
  conquer info-glut, 6–7
  cost of overload, 11–15
  handling information
    requests, 8
  organizing and storing,
    7–8
  productivity increase, 8,
    14–15
  reduce inbox overload,
    8, 15, 17–18
  reduced volume of, 8
  strategic plan 6,
  wasted time due to, 14
email block out time, 107
email challenges by vocation,
  86–87, 89, 91
email chart, 20
email etiquette, 52
email processing strategy, 47–50,
  98, 107

F

f12 key, direct save, 111
filing and finding informations,
  44, 78–79, 93, 99
filing cabinet conversion, 93
folder consistency, 92
Foster and Schrubb Financial, 2
FYI light email, 21

G

goal setting, 15–16, 38, 109, 115

H

Halsey, Vicki, 121, 129

Hamster Revolution Plan, 6, 66,
102, 130
Hamster Revolution
   training, 109
hamsterrevolution.com, 109

I

inbox, optimal number, 109
inbox, sorting, 108
incoming email, delete/store, 109
incomplete email, 22
Info-Coaching, 53
   coach self, (walking the
   walk), 55, 102
   coach others, 55
   correct email, 62
   defensiveness, 53
   example of, 65–67
   Info-Coaching Tool, 54
   lack of execution, 54
   lack of knowledge, 54
   receive coaching, 55
   target Info-Coaching, 56
   Top Ten Email Coaching
      List, 57–59
   who needs what
      Info-Coaching, 57
Info-Coaching Tool, 54
info-glut, 6–7
information storage challenges,
95-99
   mismatched folders,
   78–79
   overlapping folders, 76
   too many primary folders, 78
Instant Messaging (IM), 32,
   50, 65

K

knowledge on death row,
   101–102
Koch, Matt, 114

L

lack of execution, 54

lack of knowledge, 54
legal teams, 61
limited use of Cc, 30

M

managing information, 8
maximize folder access, 93
MikeS@hamsterrevolution.com,
   128
mismatched folder systems,
   78–80
My Documents, 86, 92–93, 111

N

needed email, 20–23
net link folders, 93
No Reply is Needed, (NRN) 29
No Thanks Needed, (NTN), 29

O

output, 84–85, 87–89, 98
organization effectiveness
team, 89
organizing and storing email,
   7–8
output, 84–85, 87–89, 98
overlapping folders, 76

P

pattern of COTA, 81–84
personal information storage,
   110–111
Power Drafts for consistency,
   92, 94
prioritize, 44, 86, 92, 98
productivity, 8, 14–15

R

reader exercise, 16, 63
redundant email, 22
reply-to-all, 14, 19, 28–29,
   31, 59
request content, 44

S

saving time, 15
search challenges, 22, 74, 79, 80, 85, 109
searchable information, 22
send less–get less, 17, 25, 30, 56, 67, 116
short replies, 47–48
Snopes.com, 27
Song, Mike, 113, 126, 128
sort email, 108
sound or visual email
  arrival, 107
storage tips, 109
strengthen the subject and sculpt the body, 42, 44
  descriptive title, 37, 44
  categories to build context
  action, 44
    brief but warm
      statement, 45
    confirmed, 43
    delivery, 43
    request, 44
synchronous communication, 29, 31-32, 108

T

targeted email, 28–33
  distribution lists, 30
  limit use of Cc, 30
  reply-to-all, 28–29
teams, 60
  executive teams, 61
  global HR team, 89
  information technology
    teams, 61
  knowledge management
    teams, 61
  legal teams, 61
teams *(Continued)*
  organization effectiveness
    team, 89
  project management teams, 61

R&D teams, 61
sales teams, 60
technology tips, 107, 130
thank-you email, 21
TimB@hamsterrevolution.com, 129
Top Ten Email Coaching List, 57–59
Top Tech Tips Newsletter, 107
Top Ten Senders List, 56–59, 63, 71

V

Vicki.halsey@kenblanchard.com, 129
virtual resume, professional image, 39–40

W

wall of words email, 39, 48
workshop content, 115

SERVICES AVAILABLE

Authors Mike Song and Tim Burress are co-founders of Cohesive Knowledge Solutions (CKS). They provide email efficiency and etiquette training, speaking, and consulting to many of the world's leading organizations. Much of The Hamster Revolution is based on CKS' landmark research and action-packed Info-Excellence Seminars.

The Info-Excellence™ Seminars
Manage Your Info Before It Manages You!

Email Efficiency & Etiquette

File & Find It Fast

Available in Live Webinar, and e-Learning Formats Individual, Team, and Orgainzation-Wide Options

Contact CKS Today and Receive a Free Email Efficiency Lesson
1-888-340-3598
www.cohesiveknowledge.com
Contact@cohesiveknowledge.com

SERVICES AVAILABLE

The Ken Blanchard Companies® is a global leader in workplace learning, productivity, performance, and leadership effectiveness that is best known for its Situational Leadership® II program—the most widely taught leadership model in the world. Because of its ability to help people excel as self-leaders and as leaders of others, SL®II is embraced by Fortune 500 companies as well as mid-to small-size businesses, governments, and educational and non-profit organizations.

Blanchard® programs—which are based on the belief that people are the key to accomplishing strategic objectives and driving business results—develop excellence in leadership, teams, customer loyalty, change management, and performance improvement. The company's continual research points to best practices for workplace improvement while its world-class trainers and coaches drive organizational and behavioral change at all levels and help people make the shift from learning to doing.

Blanchard's leadership principles are taught through interactive programs that combine 360-degree assessments, situational case studies, peer feedback, and alignment with core business objectives. Many Blanchard programs blend the use of e-learning with instructor-led training.

Leadership experts from The Ken Blanchard Companies are available for workshops, consulting, as well as keynote addresses on organizational development, workplace performance, and business trends.

Global Headquarters
The Ken Blanchard Companies
125 State Place
Escondido, CA 92029
www.kenblanchard.com
+1.800.728.6000 from the U.S.
+1.760.489.5005 from anywhere

About the Authors

Mike Song

Mike Song is one of America's leading experts on email efficiency and etiquette. A sought-after corporate trainer and keynote speaker, he's helped more than 5,000 professionals take back their lives by managing email more effectively. Mike's speaking and training engagements combine hard-hitting research, humorous stories, and hundreds of best practices to produce results. An ardent researcher, Mike has spent over five years amassing and analyzing data from more than 7,500 workplace surveys on email, information storage, and business meetings. He is co-founder and CEO of Cohesive Knowledge Solutions. Among Mike's clients are such industry leaders as Allianz, Clear Channel, Merck, Fox, HP, and Nestle. You can reach Mike at *MikeS@hamsterrevolution.com*.

Vicki Halsey, Ph.D.

Vicki Halsey is the Vice President of Applied Learning for The Ken Blanchard Companies. She is a valued presenter, keynote speaker, consultant, coach, author, and trainer, who also teaches in the MSEL program at University of San Diego. Vicki's expertise in optimal learning strategies, leadership, and blended solutions combine together as she designs and delivers innovative, high-impact leadership, and team and customer service programs. Her passion is helping professionals regain balance and meaning in their lives, so that they return home from work happy and ready to enrich the lives of their families. A partial list of Vicki's clients include: Nike, Oracle, ADP, KPMG, Nokia, Toyota, NBA, Pfizer, GAP, Merrill Lynch, Wells Fargo, Gillette, and Procter & Gamble. Vicki lives in San Diego with her two sons and husband/author, Rick. She can be contacted at *Vicki.halsey@kenblanchard.com*.

Timothy Burress

Tim Burress is the President and Sr. VP of Training for CKS. He is a talented keynote speaker and trainer. Tim has a 20-year record of excellence in sales, marketing, and training design and delivery. Before co-founding CKS in 2003, Tim was a Director of Learning and Development at Pfizer. Over the past ten years, Tim has helped over 12,000 professionals manage their information more efficiently. Tim co-developed the acclaimed Info-Excellence Seminar series, which helps teams overcome info-glut and manage information more efficiently. Tim has provided training for: Capital One, Procter & Gamble, Centex, Progressive, and Pfizer. Tim lives in Richmond Virginia with his wife Daphne and daughters Grace and Ava. Contact Tim at *TimB@hamsterrevolution.com*.

VISIT
HAMSTERREVOLUTION.COM
AND GROW!

Meet Harold and continue your journey to stress-free productivity at hamsterrevolution.com.

- Free Tech Tips, Exercises, and Newsletters.
- Hamster Revolution Productivity Tools.
- Free Hamster Revolution Discovery Center.
- Training, Speakers, and Research.
- Authors' Blog and More!
- Send a Friend or Your Entire Team!

Visit www.hamsterrevolution.com today and receive a FREE email efficiency lesson.